Better Homes and Gardens®

Style

By the Aisle

Style by the Aisle
Project Manager/Writer/Stylist: Becky Jerdee
Graphic Designer: Sundie Ruppert, Studio G
Senior Associate Design Director: Doug Samuelson
Copy Chief: Terri Fredrickson
Publishing Operations Manager: Karen Schirm
Edit and Design Production Coordinator: Mary Lee Gavin
Editorial Assistants: Kaye Chabot, Kairee Windsor
Marketing Product Managers: Aparna Pande, Isaac Petersen, Gina Rickert, Stephen Rogers, Brent Wiersma, Tyler Woods
Book Production Managers: Pam Kvitne, Marjorie J. Schenkelberg, Rick von Holdt, Mark Weaver
Contributing Copy Editor: Stacey Schildroth
Contributing Proofreaders: Beth Havey, Kathi DiNicola, Jody Speer
Cover Photographer: Marty Baldwin
Contributing Photographers: King Au, Marty Baldwin, Kim Cornelison, Hopkins Associates, Scott Little, William Stites
Indexer: Stephanie Reymann

Meredith® Books
Executive Director, Editorial: Gregory H. Kayko
Executive Director, Design: Matt Strelecki
Senior Editor/Group Manager: Vicki Leigh Ingham

Publisher and Editor in Chief: James D. Blume
Editorial Director: Linda Raglan Cunningham
Executive Director, Marketing: Jeffrey B. Myers
Executive Director, New Business Development: Todd M. Davis
Executive Director, Sales: Ken Zagor
Director, Operations: George A. Susral
Director, Production: Douglas M. Johnston
Business Director: Jim Leonard

Vice President and General Manager: Douglas J. Guendel

Better Homes and Gardens® Magazine
Editor in Chief: Karol DeWulf Nickell
Deputy Editor, Home Design: Oma Blaise Ford

Meredith Publishing Group
President: Jack Griffin
Senior Vice President: Bob Mate

Meredith Corporation
Chairman and Chief Executive Officer: William T. Kerr
President and Chief Operating Officer: Stephen M. Lacy

In Memoriam: E. T. Meredith III (1933-2003)

All of us at Meredith® Books are dedicated to providing you with information and ideas to enhance your home. We welcome your comments and suggestions. Write to us at: Meredith Books, Home Decorating Editorial Department, 1716 Locust St., Des Moines, IA 50309-3023. If you would like to purchase any of our home decorating and design, cooking, crafts, gardening, or home improvement books, check wherever quality books are sold. Or visit us at: bhgbooks.com

How to Use This Book

Whether you're a one-stop shopper, bargain hunter, or impulse buyer, you know the thrill of shopping the aisles of mass-market stores and finding a great decorating buy. In these places of "good stuff at good prices," home decor, housewares, and furniture are increasingly well-designed.

To make sense of all that good merchandise, we created *Style by the Aisle*, a directory of 15 decorating styles that walks the home furnishings aisles of mass-market stores, pulls items from the shelves, and organizes them into distinctive and personal looks you create yourself. Page through this menu of fresh, fun, and current decorating styles to select the look that suits you best. Then turn to the last two pages of each chapter for ideas on planning your decorating palette of color, pattern, and texture. Use the shopping list to focus your purchasing strategy before you actually go out to buy the furnishings.

As a handy reference, take this book on your shopping trips. The photographs identify the lines, shapes, colors, and types

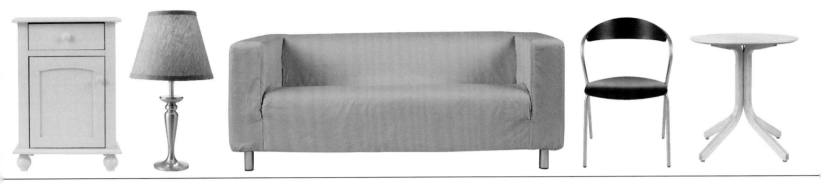

of furniture pieces you'll need. They also offer information on the kinds of accessories that complete the look. When it comes to selecting wall colors at your favorite paint store rack, you won't find paints labeled with the names you see in this book—our paint names were created to match the spirit of the style they represent and to inspire your connections to them. Use the color swatches in the book to help you select paint chips at a home improvement center or your favorite paint store.

The resource guide at the back of the book indicates where we found the items for the photos in the book. However, because merchandise changes every season or so, expect to adapt your choices to what's available and similar to what's shown, rather than to find exact duplicates.

Happy decorating,

Becky Jordee

Utility Chic

KEYS TO THE STYLE

■**EXPOSE FRAMEWORKS.** In this style walls and floors showcase the beauty of underlayments and building materials: Standard sheets of plywood and corrugated metal cover walls, and studs show through the transparent plastic-paneled walls they support. Plain drywall and subfloors wear neutral, earth colors.

■**FIND BEAUTY IN FUNCTION.** The style emphasizes utility and exposed construction. Chairs made from plywood pieces fit together like a puzzle; tables and chairs fold up or stretch out. Storage pieces, shelves, worktables, and carts wheel about for flexibility and convenience.

■**SEE THINGS AS THEY AREN'T.** Take liberties with materials and products to create new furniture. Combine a glass tabletop from one store with an upside-down galvanized bin from another to make a coffee table. Consider a metal truckbed toolbox as an end-of-the-bed storage chest.

■**BUY BASICS.** Bulk supplies of white hotel-style sheets and pillowcases, cotton blankets, bath towels, plain china, flatware, restaurant-style napkins, tablecloths, drinking glasses, and rolls of paper toweling are starting points for utility chic decorating. Massed together on open shelves and in baskets, these everyday necessities are useful and beautiful to view. Maintain the look by replenishing the stock.

■**INVENT ACCESSORIES.** Have fun with utilitarian objects. Recycle coffee cans and transparent water bottles into vases or collar a flower-filled water glass with an aluminum pipe. Pack lunches in brown paper bags and line storage shelves with wire baskets or metal paint buckets to organize small household items. Make art from building materials, cut a headboard from plywood, or "paper" a wall with sheets of sandpaper. Collect market baskets and crates to hang on walls for storage shelves or bedside stands.

PLYWOOD-CLAD WALLS CREATE A PATCHWORK BACKDROP FOR PLAINCLOTHES SEATING. A HIGH-BACKED SOFA GETS ITS
UTILITY CHIC LOOK FROM A PAINTER'S DROP CLOTH AS UPHOLSTERY. A GALVANIZED TUB TAKES A TURN AS A TABLE BASE.

Living

Settle into living spaces with utilitarian art objects and family-style comforts. Give the television set focal-point status in the room by setting it on a pedestal (stand) as if it were art. If your TV is shabby, install a flat screen on the wall or set a smaller version on a tabletop easel.

Add architecture to plain walls by combining lesser units into larger pieces. For example a restaurant shelf *right* combines with two CD racks turned sideways for a more prominent bookshelf. Aluminum elbows from the plumbing section of a home center turn into bookends while a work light hangs from the shelf as an accent light. The shelf *opposite* was built into the wall at the same time the wall was clad with sheets of plywood.

For lighting to live by, provide the room with three types: ambient, task, and accent. Ambient (overhead or general) lighting provides sufficient brightness to support the room's activities—playing games, watching television, or checking e-mail. Task lighting illuminates specific areas for activities such as reading, working at a desk, or focusing on handcrafts while you "watch" television. Accent lights draw attention to a highlight of the room, such as art. Recessed spotlights and track lights are the most common accent lights but decorative spotlights, such as can lights, also provide accents. Placed behind furniture and under plants, can lights shine up from the floor to create shadow drama on the wall. Portable and flexible, they plug into wall sockets.

ARMCHAIRS CUT FROM PLYWOOD AND SOLD IN FLAT PACKS ARE EASY TO ASSEMBLE WITHOUT TOOLS. ▲

Design dining areas for convenience and flexibility. Because form follows (fun)ction in the utility chic game, plan to rearrange and reorganize.

For everyday, eat breakfast in the kitchen and pack lunches in brown bags. Enjoy evening meals in the family room served chairside on steel TV trays that fold away on a rack when they're not in use.

For entertaining, share utility chic style with family and friends. Everyone enjoys gatherings more when they're different. Creativity, not what you spend, is key. Make a party memorable—serve a special drink, pick a theme, celebrate the first day of spring or the longest night of the year. Or try a few of these ideas: Set up a fondue potluck, make-your-own-pizza night, or have a wine, beer, or cheese tasting party. Instead of a cocktail party, throw a chocolate and champagne party.

Use buffets in several ways: for a complete meal, for drinks and hors d'oeuvres during a cocktail party, for dessert and coffee, or for an open house reception.

Arrange folding tables as needed to suit each occasion. Set tables with quality paper goods (guests will go home guiltless if you don't have to wash dishes). Arrange generous bundles of flowers in coffee or paint cans. Provide galvanized metal trash cans for party garbage and serve a platter of hot, lemon-soaked terry cloths for after-dinner hand wipes.

▲ A GLEAMING KITCHEN ISLAND ON WHEELS SERVES AS A WORKTABLE, BREAKFAST BAR, AND STORAGE UNIT.

A BAKER'S RACK WORKS AS A CHINA CUPBOARD OR A SIDEBOARD IN THE DINING ROOM. TWO 24 × 48-INCH UTILITY TABLES, PLACED END-TO-END, CREATE SEATING FOR FOUR. FOR GUESTS, ADD MORE TABLES AND FOLD THEM AWAY WHEN THEY'RE NOT IN USE. FOR FUN, COVER PLACE SETTINGS WITH STAINLESS STEEL WOK LIDS.

Dining

A BEAUTIFULLY GRAINED 4×8-FOOT SHEET OF ¾-INCH-THICK BIRCH-VENEER PLYWOOD IS CUT TO SIZE, LAID ON ITS SIDE, AND FASTENED WITH BOLTS TO A METAL BED FRAME. UTILITY LAMPS PROVIDE LIGHT FOR READING.

Sleeping

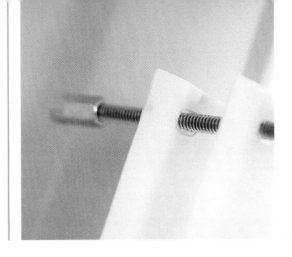

Slip to the softer side with tranquil white walls, a bed billowing with fluffy pillows and duvet, and simple bedside comforts.

PAPER SHADES WITH HOLES PUNCHED IN EACH PLEAT HANG FROM A THREADED ROD. NUTS WORK AS FINIALS. ▲

▼ FUNCTIONING HARDWARE—PULLEYS, HINGES, FERRULES, RINGS, AND BRACKETS—IS THE JEWELRY OF UTILITY CHIC.

To create the cloudlike backdrop for the bed *opposite,* sand 4×8-foot sheets of plastic (available at building centers) to give them an etched look. Attach them to wall studs with large screws and beauty washers.

Even for practical shoppers who look for basics, selecting bedding can be confusing. Thread count (threads per square inch) indicates sheet quality. A high number means finer, more tightly woven sheets. Muslin sheets with a thread count of 130 are prone to pilling; cotton or blend percales with 180 to 200 threads promise good value. While thread count is important, the quality of the thread is important too. A 280-count sheet with poor thread quality may not be as comfortable as a 200-count sheet with good-quality thread. Top-quality sheets, such as pima or Egyptian cotton, have extralong, lustrous fibers. Lay your cheek against the material for an indication of quality and comfort.

The ideal duvet (a down- or feather-filled comforter with a woven fabric cover) measures at least 18 inches wider than the bed and provides lightweight, self-adjusting warmth. While not as warm or natural, nonallergenic down cotton or wool alternatives are available.

Details make a difference

Bookmobile ▲

SEE A PLANT DOLLY FOR WHAT IT ISN'T—A LIBRARY ON WHEELS. WITH A SMALL STACK OF BOOKS, IT ROLLS AROUND ON A TABLETOP LIKE A LAZY SUSAN. CHAIRSIDE, IT HOLDS A COLLECTION OF READING MATERIALS PILED HIGH WITH OVERSIZE VOLUMES. THE TOP BOOK ON THE BOOKMOBILE BECOMES A TABLETOP.

Clip Art ▲

BE CLEVER. SEPARATE A SERIES FROM A MULTI-IMAGE POSTER AND HAVE THEM LAMINATED AT A PRINT SHOP. TRIM THE IMAGES, LEAVING ¼-INCH MARGINS. USE MAGNETIC CLIPS TO DISPLAY THEM ON A METAL CABINET.

Soft Spot ▲

CREATE SOFT PLACES TO FALL. THE HARD
EDGES OF UTILITY CHIC REQUIRE PILLOWS
FOR BODILY COMFORT, AND THESE
24-INCH-SQUARE FLOOR PILLOWS OFFER
CUSHY CLOSE-TO-THE-GROUND SEATING.
SHOP FOR HARD-WEARING FABRICS, SUCH
AS BURLAP, AND STURDY STRIPED
UPHOLSTERY FABRICS TO SEW CUSHION
COVERS YOURSELF (NOTE THE NOTCHED
CORNERS ON THE PILLOWS *ABOVE*). OR
BUY READY-MADE FLOOR CUSHIONS.

Picture-Hanging Pulleys ▲

HANG PICTURES FROM PULLEYS WITH
CABLE. FOR EACH PICTURE, DRIVE TWO
SCREW EYES INTO THE TOP EDGE OF THE
FRAME. SLIP A FERRULE OVER ONE END
OF A LENGTH OF CABLE, THEN PASS THE
CABLE THROUGH THE FIRST SCREW EYE.
SLIDE THE FERRULE OVER THE CABLE
END TO SECURE IT. THREAD THE FREE
END OF THE CABLE THROUGH A PULLEY
AND SECURE IT TO THE OTHER SCREW
EYE IN THE SAME WAY. DRIVE A SCREW
HOOK INTO YOUR WALL AND ADD AN S
HOOK. HANG THE PULLEY FROM THE S
HOOK. FOR CONSISTENT RESULTS WHEN
HANGING A ROW OF PICTURES, CUT
CABLE PIECES THE SAME LENGTH.

Planning the Look

COLOR Gather paint chips and wood stains from a paint store using the color strip *above* as a guide. Establish a color palette by selecting two of the colors for painting your walls and woodwork. Keep the rest of the colors in hand as you shop for coordinating fabrics and furnishings.

PATTERN When choosing upholstery, window treatments, or soft furnishings, think plain, striped, and plaid. Black and tan stripes create bold patterning in a room while two shades of gold or khaki deliver a muted look. Scan the aisles for overall patterns on rugs, upholstery fabric, or pillow coverings. To contrast overall striped patterns, look for slim borders of fine stripes on plain linens or graphic plaids on everyday dish towels or blankets.

TEXTURE In a muted, neutral color scheme with few patterns and many plain-colored surfaces, texture is key to creating visual excitement in a room. Contrast the smooth sheen of stainless steel with the roughness of burlap and sisal. Play hammered metal against slippery vinyl; combine glass with galvanized metal. Uncover the ribs of a coffee can, the softness of down, the spiraled ends of journals, and the tongues-and-grooves of car siding. If you've opted for a bold, graphic look, the need for texture isn't as important.

SISAL | HAMMERED ALUMINUM | HEAVY WOVEN COTTONS

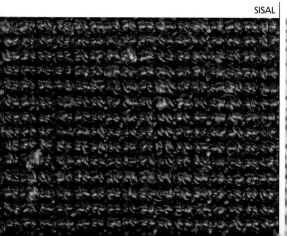
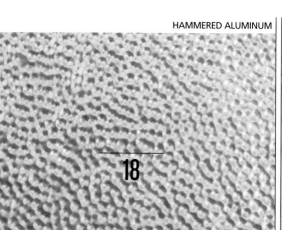
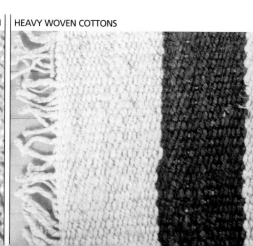

What to Shop for

FURNITURE straight-lined sofa upholstered in washable canvas or painter's drop cloth │ folding metal chairs │ metal, plywood, or plastic chairs and bar-height stools with exposed frames │ vinyl, metal, stainless-steel, or plywood tables │ utility shelving │ rolling baker's racks and pantry carts │ plywood, metal, or concrete-block bedside, coffee, and side tables

WINDOW TREATMENTS pleated paper shades │ roller shades │ standard white sheers hung on tension rods │ hinged pine shutters with pulleys │ white cafe curtains hung on cable wire "curtain rods" │ metal miniblinds

SOFT FURNISHINGS white cotton duvets, sheets, pillowcases, tablecloths, and napkins │ terry cloth bath towels and bath mats │ ticking, canvas, burlap, and burlaplike upholstery fabrics for toss- or floor-pillow coverings │ cotton dish towels, unpatterned paper supplies │ sisal, coir, or cotton rugs

TABLETOP FURNISHINGS plain white china, bulk paper plates and napkins │ stainless-steel flatware, pots, pans, and chargers │ standard clear glasses and stemware │ generic food and water supplies │ black place mats

LIGHTING cable lighting │ work lights │ photo or basketball lights (bulbs covered with wire nets) │ bare-bulb art lamps (see page 11) │ track lights

STRIPE PATTERNS | BLACK-WHITE PLAIDS | HARDWOOD FLOORINGS | STRIPED BORDERS

China Blue

KEYS TO THE STYLE

■ **SIMPLIFY YOUR HOME** with an Asian aesthetic. The minimalism and natural motifs of this style go hand-in-hand with today's trend toward pale colors, dark woods, and clean lines. Borrow landscape through open windows with treatments that roll up for a clear view. Replace heavy carpets with easy-to-clean terrazzo, tile, bamboo, light wood, or laminate flooring.

■ **NEUTRALIZE SETTINGS** with light paint on walls and window treatments of matchstick or bamboo blinds, breezy white cotton curtain panels, plain sheers, or rice paper roll-ups. On smooth, shiny floors, spread out import-store area rugs of sisal, hemp, dark bamboo, or rush.

■ **RECLINE ON UPHOLSTERY** covered with plain, neutral fabrics that have interesting weaves or textures. Choose long, low seating that fits the zenlike atmosphere inspired by Buddhism. Sleep on low platforms or, for western comfort, beds at a normal height.

■ **SIT ON BAMBOO** and cane chairs or on floor cushions carefully arranged on rush mats. Divide rooms with rice paper or woven bamboo floor screens. This highly organized aesthetic values a lack of clutter and condensed storage. Put away everything not in use, stowing items in chests of drawers, armoires, low chests, buffets, and stacked baskets.

■ **ACCENT WITH BLUE** and white. Inject lively focal points in serene settings with imported porcelains and fabrics as well as a few domestic pieces resembling the Asian aesthetic. Brighten neutral seating pieces with blue and white patterned cushions and throws. Zap a white wall with a kimono hanging. Paint bamboo dining chairs China Sea blue or hang blue and white paper lanterns over the dining room table. Only a few shots of blue in each room do the trick.

TO SEE BLUE'S POWER TO GRACE NEUTRAL SPACES WITH
VITALITY, IMAGINE THIS ARMOIRE WITHOUT A DISPLAY OF
PORCELAINS AND THE SOFA WITHOUT CUSHIONS.

Living

Decorating with a China Blue focus requires restraint and a desire for simplicity. Uncluttered living—an aesthetic borrowed from Asia—brings serenity to rooms where you can relax with a book, host a friendly gathering, or simply sit in the space and gaze out the window.

Begin with neutral walls and smooth, clean floors. Think neutral when it comes to purchasing living room furniture. Buy western-style upholstered seating and armchairs to suit western-style comfort levels. Add Asian-style benches, storage pieces, armchairs, baskets, and tables to give the room the authenticity of Chinese lines, character, and materials. You'll find plenty of options in mass-market stores and import stores that offer "Made-in-China" items.

China Blue is all about taking an understated, blank canvas of a room with neutral furniture and giving it a one-two punch of indigo blue. Because blue is a strong color, especially in a neutral room, you'll need only a little of it. Save blue for energizing focal points, such as a bouquet on a dark wood coffee table, screen-printed cushions on a cream-color sofa, and porcelain on the empty shelf in a bamboo armoire. Define an entrance with a door drape. Bring vibrancy to a blank wall with a framed batik, a poster, or a printed cotton bathrobe you find while shopping for groceries at a Chinese market. For a delicate balance of texture and fragrance, float a flower in a blue and white porcelain bowl of water.

A SINGLE BLUE KIMONO, HUNG ON A BAMBOO ROD, IS ALL THE FOCUS THIS ENTRY NEEDS. ▲

Grace your tables with still life studies in blue and white. Setting the table is part of the dining ritual, a time for ephemeral decorating. Invent new centerpieces from a collection of porcelain pots, hang textiles to dramatize a meal, and serve food with an easy spirit.

Inside or out, China Blue dining rooms exude an air of relaxed elegance. Cleared off, tables are empty canvases waiting for table-setting experimentation. To inspire decorating, supply yourself with the tools and materials for arranging China Blue tables. Scout import stores for blue and white porcelain dishes. Collect a blue and white palette of table coverings from various sources. Include basics like white hotel-style tablecloths.

Invest in good storage. In the kitchen use cabinets with doors that close over anything that detracts from the blue, white, and bamboo aesthetic. Stack dishes and bamboo platters or steamers in plain view on open shelves and arrange linens and flatware in boxes and woven baskets. Storage options in the dining room include buffets, china cupboards, and bamboo chests.

Decorate walls with light paneling or paint and dress windows with airy curtain panels. If the spirit moves you, paint bamboo chairs blue to give the dining room a welcoming splash of cool color.

When the time comes, snip fresh greenery for the table and display it in your most valued porcelain pots. Invent new ways to use greenery on place settings for parties.

▲ BLUE AND WHITE TABLECLOTHS AND A SARONG TIED TO A BRANCH INVITE DINING IN A BAMBOO GROVE.

BATTERY-OPERATED PARTY LIGHTS AND PAPER GLOBES HANG BY WHITE STRINGS OVER A VISUAL FEAST OF BLUE AND WHITE IMPORT-STORE PORCELAINS. FLOOR-TO-CEILING STRIPED PANELS HUNG AT INTERVALS EXAGGERATE THE HEIGHT OF THE SPACE. SHEERS AT THE WINDOWS ALLUDE TO INVITING OUTDOOR SPACES BEYOND.

Dining

IN A WHITE SETTING, CHINA BLUE PATTERNS POP A SLEEPING SPACE WITH WIDE-AWAKE DESIGNS. FABRICS WITH BLUE TIE-DYE ON A WHITE BACKGROUND PACK LESS PUNCH THAN THE TWO PILLOWS WITH SMALL WHITE PATTERNS SET ON STRONG BACKGROUNDS OF DEEP INDIGO BLUE.

Sleeping

Make beds of tranquility in white spaces blessed with blue and white textiles. Bring a sense of well-being to your private haven with tea service, the soft light of paper lamps, and greenery from the garden.

Feng shui, the ancient Chinese art of putting things in their place, offers these commonsense tips for creating the right energy flow in your bedroom: Place the head of the bed on the wall facing the door. Allow a 30-inch-wide corridor on at least one side of the bed. Hang a mirror anywhere but opposite your bed—your reflection could wake you from a restful state. Balance the weights of storage pieces in the room. After placing the bed, put the largest piece in the largest remaining space. Place the smallest pieces last. Ban TV, computer, and excercise equipment. If you can't, hide them in an armoire or behind a screen so you can get your rest. Soften windowpanes with green plants.

PARED-DOWN ACCESSORIZING FOCUSES ATTENTION ON A FEW GREAT FURNITURE PIECES. ▲

Tabletop Blues ▲

TURN A BLUE-TRIMMED BEACH MAT INTO A DINING
ROOM TABLE RUNNER. THEN LAY 5-INCH SQUARES OF
ORIGAMI PAPER AT INTERVALS ALONG THE RUNNER'S
EDGES AS A TEMPORARY TABLE COVERING. YOU'LL
FIND ORIGAMI PAPERS IN ART AND CRAFTS SUPPLY
STORES AND BEACH MATS IN IMPORT STORES.

Spa Tray ▲

UPDATE TOWELS WITH CHINA BLUES AND NEW DISPLAY TECHNIQUES.
FOLD TUB AND SHOWER NEEDS INTO A DARK WOOD TRAY WITH LOW,
ASIAN LINES.

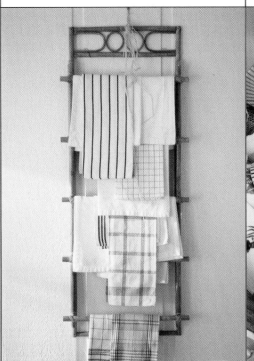

Everyday Linens ▲

LAYER BLUE AND WHITE DISH TOWELS AND NAPKINS ON A BAMBOO RACK HUNG ON THE WALL WITH A RAFFIA TIE. ORDINARY AMERICAN DOMESTIC LINENS IN STRIPES, PLAIDS, CHECKS, AND SOLIDS MAKE GOOD DECORATING COMPANIONS FOR PORCELAINS MADE IN CHINA.

China Blue Patterns ▲

A WEALTH OF BLUE AND WHITE DISHES WAIT ON IMPORT-STORE RACKS. TO DISTINGUISH CHINESE PORCELAINS FROM EUROPEAN IMPORTS (GERMAN, ITALIAN, AND PORTUGUESE) CHECK LABELS AND COMPARE THE PATTERN DIFFERENCES. CHINESE PORCELAINS ARE SIMILAR TO JAPANESE PIECES BUT HAVE LOOSER FLOWER, FISH, STRIPE, AND CHINESE ZODIAC DESIGNS. YOU'LL ALSO FIND COMBINATIONS OF OVERALL PATTERNS LIKE THESE *ABOVE*.

Planning the Look

COLOR A happy marriage of two colors, blue and white are an easy-to-use decorating duo. For this style, eliminate all other hues from your plans. Collect a variety of blue paint chips and fabric swatches to recognize the wide range of blues from violet to green. For a China Blue scheme, select "true blues" and slightly violet blues to pair with whites and other neutrals.

PATTERN The most important feature of this style is blue and white patterning that resembles the Asian aesthetic. Gather knowledge of Chinese patterning by visiting import stores and starting a collection of small soup bowls and linens that speak to you. Look for free-form tie-dyed, painted, or batiked fish, flowers, leaves, and Chinese zodiac designs as well as organized stripes, dots, plaids, and nonobjective shapes. Plan to use these patterns judiciously as focal points so they don't overturn the serenity of your rooms.

TEXTURE Base rooms on large areas of neutral-colored textures that create quiet backdrops. Lay rustic hemp or sisal on smooth floors. Buy upholstery with canvas, duck, or leather covers. Invest in paper-thin surfaces, breezy sheers, woven bamboo, raffia flourishes, and brass hinges. Contrast smooth porcelains with crinkly seersuckers, thirsty terry cloths, and rough cottons.

ORIGAMI PAPER | BAMBOO FLOORING | WAVE PATTERNS

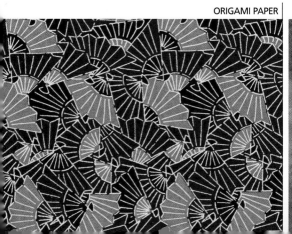

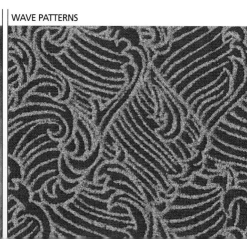

What to Shop for

▼

FURNITURE bamboo or upholstered sofas with neutral covers | folding or stationary bamboo and cane chairs | futons or standard beds with metal frames | dark or light wood dining tables, armoires, tansu chests, buffets, nesting tables, and floor screens | white laminate chests of drawers and shelving units with doors | stacking storage baskets with lids

WINDOW TREATMENTS rice paper roll-up shades | matchstick or bamboo roll-up or Roman blinds | standard white sheers with side panels of blue and white patterning | white shutters | floor screens | wood-slat blinds

SOFT FURNISHINGS blue and white sarongs, tablecloths, duvets, sheets, pillowcases, dish towels, and napkins | terry cloth towels with blue patterning | ticking, canvas, and blue and white printed upholstery fabrics for toss or floor cushions | rush beach mats | rush or wood mats, sisal area rugs

TABLETOP FURNISHINGS blue and white "Made-in-China" porcelain bowls, plates, platters, cups, and vases | stainless-steel flatware, pots, and pans | bamboo steamers | origami papers | clear glasses and stemware

LIGHTING cable lighting | floor and table lamps with paper shades | bamboo lanterns | bamboo/paper lanterns | recessed lighting

STYLIZED FLOWERS | CERAMIC TILES | MATCHSTICK | TIE-DYE

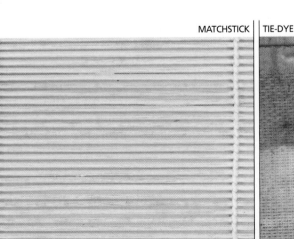

New Country

KEYS TO THE STYLE

■ **WHITEWASH SURFACES.** To create new country style, paint walls, floors, and moldings white to develop a white envelope of space. For textural appeal add beadboard or clapboard panels to walls or hang panels of fabric as room dividers. Leave windows uncovered to showcase the window frames and allow the flow of natural light.

■ **BUY WHITE STORAGE PIECES.** Dressers, cupboards, and bookcases blend into the whitewashed backdrop and become part of the white envelope of space. Similarly, white tables are part of the stationary architecture that welcomes the colorful, movable parts of the room.

■ **PUNCH IT UP.** Look on the bright side when selecting chairs, sofa slipcovers, bed and table coverings, lamps, side tables, rugs, or dishes. Pure, clear colors—think orange, pink, yellow, green, and aqua—rev up the new country world and bring vitality and livability to quiet white spaces.

■ **BE CLUTTER-FREE.** Stick to the basics and avoid unnecessary accessorizing that takes you back to country styles of the past. This country style is modern and minimal with a clear-cut vision of simplicity. Adopt this mantra to keep hoarding habits in line: When something new comes into the room, something old goes out. Send the item to another room, another home, or to a yard sale. Less is more.

■ **BRING NATURE INSIDE.** For special occasions or everyday celebrations that warrant a colorful flurry or two, go with countryside flowers and orchard fruit. In a whitewashed setting, color is powerful and you need only a few well-chosen hues to reap a feel-good benefit. Use a single flower in a slim vase or a single flower in each of three vases. For a big bouquet, stick to a single type of flower, such as spider mums, carnations, tulips, or hydrangeas. For a fruit bowl, use one kind in a color that contrasts with other colors in the room. Mass for impact.

A NEW READY-TO-ASSEMBLE DESK, LOOKING OUT ON THE COUNTRYSIDE THROUGH CURTAINLESS WINDOWS, BECOMES PART OF THE WHITEWASHED BACKDROP. A BRIGHT CHAIR, LAMP, AND RAG RUGS ENERGIZE THE WORK SPACE.

Living

Stripped down to bare essentials, decorating the new country way is about minimal rules that bring on maximum comfort and livability.

While a sofa is the basis for a new country living room, its companion, the white coffee table, plays host. Modern by all appearances, it anchors the room, offering shelving and dining service to those seated around it. In new country opposites attract, mixing contemporary sofas with traditional wooden or wicker chairs. Or the reverse could be true: a traditional sofa paired with contemporary armchairs. If the contradictory style appeals to you but you're not ready to fully jump in, practice pairing opposites with small investments, such as table or desktop pieces. Add a few pieces at a time to work with your living room of the future. Turn the page for more opposing ideas to try.

COLORFUL FARMHOUSE CHAIRS MOVE ABOUT EASILY FOR CONVERSATION AROUND A COFFEE TABLE. ▲

Dare to be spare. Just a few splashes of color energize whitewashed dining spaces. They also inspire the appetite and punch up a party.

The core of country dining is a hospitable table—it can be rectangular, square, or round. An architectural element in the room, a white table speaks the language of new country style: clean, fresh, and brand-new. A round one is often a favorite choice for country-style dining because conversation is easier when guests are gathered in a circle than when they're lined up along a rectangular table. Choose any white table with good lines, such as patio plastic, metal foldouts, straight-lined wooden tables to assemble yourself, or unfinished pieces you can paint. For other architectural pieces in the room, such as hutches, sideboards, or cupboards, choose white ones to blend into the walls and show off high-color tableware.

To bring the white space to life, add pure, unabashedly childlike colors. Buy a wardrobe of country-mod tablecloths and napkins. Score bargains at clearance sales for plates, bowls, and platters that resemble vintage Fiestaware. In the spring you'll find happy, graphic dot-, stripe-, or plaid-design plastics in store aisles promoting picnicware. Check furniture aisles for stick-back farm chairs you can paint in saturated colors. Pick up woven rag rugs to scatter or lay down as runners. Tip: Put self-adhesive felt cushions on the ends of chair legs to keep them from scratching white-painted flooring.

▲ STICK-BACK CHAIRS IN EYE-POPPING COLORS MAKE FOR CHOOSE-YOUR-CHAIR FUN AT MEALS.

BRAND-NEW WINDSOR CHAIRS LOOK LIKE OLD ONES BUT DON'T COME AT ANTIQUE PRICES. THEY'RE PAINTED A BRILLIANT ▼
FUCHSIA AND CIRCLE ABOUT A GENEROUS, ROUND PATIO TABLE. A MINIMALIST CENTERPIECE OF ONE ORANGE VASE AND
A GIANT PLATTER OF ORANGES CREATES A SHARP FOCUS.

Dining

THIS NEW COUNTRY QUILT IS HAND-STITCHED, COMPLETELY WASHABLE, AND AS COMFORTABLE AS A CLOUD. ONCE ASSEMBLED, THE FLAT-PACK HEADBOARD IS PLACED NEAR A WINDOW FOR THE BEST OUTDOOR VIEW.

Sleeping

Surround yourself in a peaceful atmosphere of white walls, floors, and storage pieces. Then inject the new country vibe with lively linens, flowers, and rugs.

To create a serene sleeping space, whitewash the room to welcome and reflect a natural flow of light through uncovered windows. If privacy is an issue, add white sheers, shutters, or white-wood blinds you can adjust for light control or close for privacy. Place the bed perpendicular to or facing the windows for the first view of the sun in the morning and the last stargazing at night. (If your view is urban, think of the city lights as bright stars.)

Consider new possibilities for a headboard, the furniture focal point around which all other bedroom elements are placed. You could go with a traditional ready-to-assemble headboard—a vertical panel that keeps pillows from falling off at the head of the bed—or transform a large dresser into a headboard. Placed with its back to the head of the bed near the center of a room, a dresser anchors an island for sleep. Drawers are accessible by walking around the island and bed making is easy on both sides. If you have a tape measure, a level, a hammer, and a few screwdrivers, you can buy flat-packed, ready-to-assemble furniture pieces, such as the ones shown on these pages, and build them yourself. Tip: If the back of the dresser is unattractive, paint it to match the front of the dresser. Or cover it with fabric or wallcovering.

A FLAT-PACK DRESSER WORKS AS A HEADBOARD FOR A BED PLACED IN THE MIDDLE OF THE ROOM. ▲

Details make a difference

Mantel Pieces ▲

START A COLLECTION OF NEW CERAMICS. CONTRAST THE SLICK, SMOOTH SURFACES OF SHORT AND SQUAT GLAZED CERAMIC VASES AGAINST ROUGH WHITE WOOD WALLS FOR THE VISUAL THRILL OF IT.

Chair Art ▲

BE AN ARTIST. IN AN AIRY, WHITE SPACE FILLED WITH REFLECTIVE SURFACES AND WHITE FURNISHINGS, ADD A BRILLIANT STROKE OF COLOR WITH A PANEL OF FABRIC OR A SHAPELY PAINTED CHAIR.

Rag Rug Riches ▲

LINE A ROOM WITH LUXURY. EVERY HOME FURNISHINGS STORE HAS A TREASURE TROVE OF SMALL RAG RUGS AT LOW PRICES. BUY ENOUGH TO MAKE A LARGE AREA RUG TO FEEL THE EASE OF CARPET BENEATH YOUR FEET. TO MAKE THE RUG, STITCH SEVERAL RUGS TOGETHER WITH FABRIC STORE CARPET THREAD OR FASTEN THEM IN PLACE ON THE FLOOR WITH DOUBLE-FACED CARPET TAPE. PRACTICE THE LAYOUT ON THE FLOOR BEFORE FASTENING THE RUGS TOGETHER. FOR AN EVEN ARRANGEMENT, YOU'LL NEED RUGS THAT ARE EXACTLY THE SAME SIZE. FOR RUGS OF VARIOUS SIZES, USE A STAGGERED LAYOUT.

Bamboo Surprise ▲

BRING HOME A COUNTRY ARMCHAIR PAINTED AND DRESSED IN MANGO TO JOLT A BLAND WHITE INTERIOR OUT OF ITS BOREDOM. COMBINE IT WITH STANDARD WHITE WICKER TO MAKE A FOCAL POINT IN A SEATING ARRANGEMENT OR LET IT STAND ALONE AS A PLEASING ELEMENT AGAINST A WHITE-CURTAINED BACKDROP.

| GRASS GREEN | BLUE HYDRANGEA | HOT GOLD | MANDARIN ORANGE | BLAZE RED |

Planning the Look

▼

COLOR Ready to take the new country leap? Choose a basic white—a warm ivory or a cool dove white—to use as the standard color for your entire house. Use it to paint walls, woodwork, and floors. A consistent white from room to room brings unity to your interior while it envelops the spaces, creating a backdrop to emphasize high-color country. Using the colors *above* gather saturated paint chips for referral while shopping for furnishings or paint.

PATTERN Accent fabrics with bold floral prints or geometrics on white backgrounds set new country style apart from the past. A bit old country, but mostly contemporary, the mix is fresh and up-to-date. Sometimes a room begins with a patterned fabric, such as a pair of punchy pillows that inspires a plain-color sofa slipcover (page 35). Or a bedroom starts with a fun floral rug (page 38) that leads to the purchase of a quilt with bold stripes in similar colors.

TEXTURE Hallmarks of country style—torn edges, frayed fringes, quirky quilt surfaces, smooth ironstone, enamelware, rough barn boards, and grooved beadboard—translate easily into new country style with brand-new items from the aisles of stores. New country style means new imported quilts, hot-off-the-loom lace curtains, new "rag" rugs, smooth paneling, and unchipped china.

| HAND-STITCHED TEXTURES | BOLD FLORAL PRINTS | TORN EDGES | COTTON FRINGES |

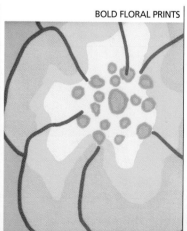

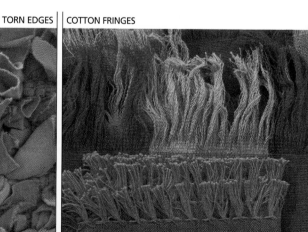

What to Shop for

FURNITURE straight-lined, rolled-arm, or camelback sofa with washable plain-colored slipcovers | wingbacks, Windsor chairs, wicker or wooden chairs with spindle backs to paint in bright colors, porch swings | square, round, gateleg, or long, wooden harvest tables | ready-to-assemble storage pieces with white finishes (lingerie chests, dressers, headboards, nightstands, china cupboards, bookcases, and mirrors) | white patio, coffee, or side tables

WINDOW TREATMENTS white sheers or cotton duck drapes on white wood rods | white wood shutters or blinds | white lace or plain cafe curtains

SOFT FURNISHINGS bright-colored cotton quilts, comforters, duvet covers, sheets, pillowcases, place mats, bath towels, and bath mats | rag, shag, or pile rugs | dish towels, tablecloths, and napkins with modern plaid, check, stripe, or dot designs | wool plaid throws, graphic floral-print toss pillows

TABLETOP FURNISHINGS white and bright plain-colored china, chargers, vases, pitchers, and bowls | stainless-steel or enamelware pots and pans | clear-glass drinking glasses, bowls, and stemware | fruit, wildflowers

LIGHTING cable lighting | ginger jar table lamps | contemporary stainless-steel lamps or chandeliers | lanterns | track lights

TWO-COLOR FLORAL DESIGNS | WHITE-PAINTED FLOOR PLANKS | WOVEN TEXTURES | IMPRESSIONISTIC FLOWERS

Isle Style

KEYS TO THE STYLE

■**LIVE IN THE ZONE** between indoors and out—the transitional roofed space that's connected to your house but left open on at least one side. Think veranda, porch, patio, terrace, or a narrow aisle of shade under an overhang. Even in northern climates, these semi-protected areas can be turned into tropical isles for living.

■**BLEND INDOORS AND OUT** with sheers and shutters at your windows. Keep indoor rooms airy, uncrowded by clutter, and open to the view outdoors. Decorate rooms with lush, green tropical plants. Consider adding a porch or greenhouse, or expanding rooms with bow and bay windows.

■**LIE LOW,** leaving horizontal spaces for relaxing on long sofas, daybeds, and chaises. Hang hammocks or swings. Create outdoor living and cooking spaces that can be quickly covered or stored when bad weather shows up. Keep stackable chairs nearby for drop-in company.

■**MIX NATURAL MATERIALS** for a variety of textures: woven sisal or straw rugs, smooth ceramic-tiled floors, fine linen bedspreads, smooth cotton or silk sheets, airy mosquito net canopies and curtains, rope hammocks, rough mudcloth cushions, rush mats, soft tie-dyed sarongs, silk ribbon door drapes, hopsack upholstery, batik cotton toss pillows, vinyl table coverings, wicker seating, and carved mahogany.

■**TAKE A BROAD VIEW** when choosing accessories, integrating the British Colonial, African, and native Caribbean decorative influences of the past. Find them in current island style items designed by mass market manufacturers. Shopping is particularly good in the spring when stores set out leisure-time items for patio dining, summer sleeping, and outdoor living.

A LOGGIA, OPEN ON ONE SIDE, IS THE PERFECT PLACE FOR ISLE STYLE LIVING. VINES AND FLOWERS SOFTEN HARD CONCRETE EDGES, CREATING A BOWER OF BEAUTY. LIGHTWEIGHT FURNITURE MOVES ASIDE EASILY WHEN IT RAINS.

Living

Isle style living happens mostly in the middle zone—that shady aisle of open space that expands the size of your house and offers you room to breathe. Tap into the casual life by furnishing a balcony, patio, or any outdoor space that protects you from the sun and rain.

The typical tropical living space is created by circling a large number of chairs around a small central table. Although the table isn't particularly accessible to each chair, no one seems to mind—like the hub of a wheel holding spokes, the table pulls together a circle of friends. Chairs (not heavy sofas) move easily about to accommodate any number of occupants in the open space.

For isle style living choose a round "coffee table"—a downturned basket, a 3-legged side table, or a decorator table with a pretty skirt and a glass top—and place it at the center of the mid-zone space. Group lightweight cane, bamboo or wood seating pieces that can quickly be moved to a protected area during a storm. Weatherproof wicker is a good option that assures less wear and tear from the elements. Soften seats with removable seat and back cushions in isle style prints and patterns. For mildew- and moisture-resistant cushions choose fabrics manufactured specifically for outdoor use.

In the evening, light the space with candles in lanterns, strings of electric lights hung overhead, or torches on sticks inserted into the ground at the side of the room.

DIRECTOR'S CHAIRS FOLD UP FOR EASY TRANSPORT TO POOL, BEACH, OR GARDEN SPOTS. ▲

Isle style is all about flexibility. Indulge in al fresco dining whenever weather obliges—the intoxications of pure light and fresh air increase the appetite. When it storms, eat inside at an impromptu table.

All meals vary from one to the next—no menu is exactly the same, and the number of people at the table may change. Isle style dining adds another variation: the place where a meal is served. Some meals can be enjoyed outside, others are best inside the house. Create a variety of locations for dining in and around your isle-style home.

For dining inside set up tables in several locations: in the dining room, in the living room on a round table that doubles as a desk, in the kitchen at a bar-height table, or in a bedroom as if it were room service at a seaside hotel. If weather permits, spread out on a three-season porch, patio, balcony, or terrace. To block the hot afternoon sun and make a space seem more private, hang a panel of outdoor fabric from the roof.

Accent lighting that focuses softly on the table creates an atmosphere for dining and promotes lingering. One indoor option is an import-store paper globe on a light cord. Attach it to a corded fixture with a bulb that hangs from a hook in the ceiling and plugs into a wall socket. Another idea: Paint a chandelier white, add colorful shades, and fit it with a dimmer switch. For outdoor dining hang lanterns from trees to add ephemeral beauty to meals.

CHECK PARTY STORES FOR ISLAND-INSPIRED VOTIVE HOLDERS, LANTERNS ON ELECTRICAL CORDS, AND TABLEWARE.

THIS OUTDOOR DINING ROOM IS VIRTUALLY WEATHERPROOF—WITH THE EXCEPTION OF THE PAPER PLATES. DURABLE MARINE PAINT COVERS THE HANDMADE TABLE AND WOODEN STOOLS. ▼

Dining

A CARIBBEAN-STYLE PAINTED HEADBOARD, BRIGHT AFRICAN-MOTIF FABRICS, AND A WEST INDIES INSPIRED LAMP COMBINE IN A TROPICAL SYNTHESIS OF DIFFERENT CULTURES. WHITE COTTON AND WICKER PULSE AGAINST THE WATERY COLORS, CREATING AN UNMISTAKABLE ISLE STYLE VIBE.

Sleeping

Swing, sway, or slip into a blissful sleep with the sound of waves—even if it means a track on your CD player. Make your bed anywhere you please.

For isle style bedding shop store aisles in late spring and early summer. Fashions change seasonally, and trendy experimental designs appear for use in warm-weather months. Look for free-spirited tie-dye or batik toss pillows and bedcoverings. Purchase hotel-white sheets and pillowcases to contrast with bright-colored fabrics. For a British Colonial Caribbean look, hang an import-store mosquito net canopy over a dark wood poster bed dressed in all-white bedding. For a relaxing day away, set up an open-air pavilion or a sleeping cabana. You'll need a beach umbrella, a white, heat-reflecting tent, or a shade made from a sheet raised on four tent poles through large grommets at each corner.

BATIK PILLOWS AND A "SHEET" MADE FROM YARDAGE SWING LOW IN A HAMMOCK OVER THE INCOMING TIDE. ▲

Details make a difference

Wave Lamp ▲

ADD ISLE STYLE TO A DISCOUNT STORE FABRIC SHADE WITH A FREEHAND WAVE DESIGN PAINTED WITH BLUE AND GREEN ACRYLIC PAINT.

Painted Cupboard ▲

SPICE UP AN UNFINISHED CABINET WITHOUT HIDING THE GRAIN BY USING WOOD DYES. YOU CAN CONTROL THE HUE'S INTENSITY, FROM SEMITRANSPARENT TO NEARLY OPAQUE. TO GET THE TRANSPARENCY YOU WANT, ADD SOLVENTS ACCORDING TO THE PRODUCT DIRECTIONS.

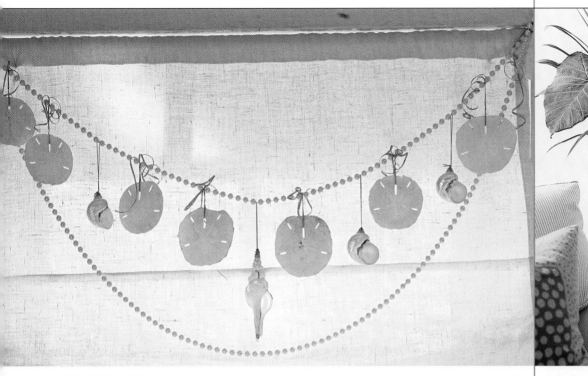

Shell Necklace ▲

MAKE JEWELRY FOR YOUR WINDOWS. FASTEN TWO STRANDS OF WHITE CHRISTMAS TREE PEARL GARLAND AT THE TOP OF A WINDOW FRAME OVER A WHITE LINEN SHADE. TIE SAND DOLLARS AND SHELL CHRISTMAS TREE ORNAMENTS ON THE TOP PEARL STRAND WITH STRING OR NARROW RIBBON.

Green Bouquets ▲

TROPICAL PLANTS YIELD LARGE, SHAPELY LEAVES. FOR DRAMATIC AND INEXPENSIVE DISPLAYS, CUT SINGLE STALKS FROM TROPICAL PLANTS TO PLACE IN COOL, WHITE CERAMIC VASES. IN NORTHERN CLIMATES AFFORDABLE TROPICAL PLANTS CAN BE FOUND IN GARDEN STORES YEAR-ROUND. KEEP A FEW PLANTS IN A SOLARIUM OR FOUR-SEASON PORCH FOR CUTTING.

Planning the Look

COLOR
Think bright, hot, and saturated. Plan to use pure white to make the vibrant colors vibrate more. Also insert a touch of black with white for even more zing and splash. Check the interior design section of your favorite bookstore for Caribbean-style decorating books to inspire your palette and inform your purchasing choices.

PATTERN
When choosing architectural trims, seat cushions, toss pillows, and bedding, keep in mind the variety of cultures that make up the history of island life: native chevrons, stripes, and squares; British Colonial fretwork, chintz, lace, and Asian rugs; African mudcloths, batiks, and tie-dye patterns inspired by seashells, birds, and exotic flowers; and Creole arabesques and scrolls.

TEXTURE
Indulge your senses in a contrast of textures to celebrate the exuberant, over-the-top attitude of isle style. Carry smooth, manufactured plastic dishes on a rough-finished wooden tray. Combine wicker furniture pieces in rooms with smooth, ceramic-tiled floors. Float a frail mosquito net canopy over a dark, mahogany poster bed. Lay sisal area rugs on shiny wood floor planks. Circle shiny, metal chairs around a table covered in seersucker fabric. Place a metal coffee server on a lace-covered table.

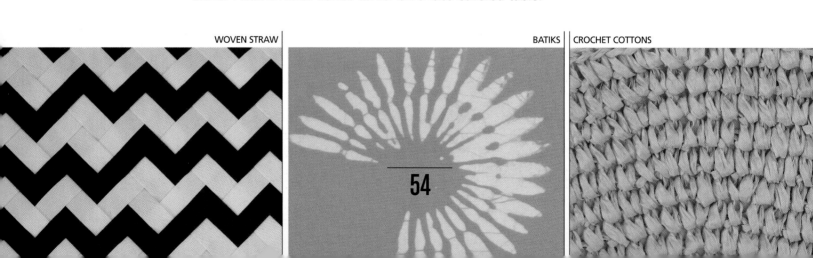

WOVEN STRAW | | | BATIKS | CROCHET COTTONS

What to Shop for

FURNITURE plantation chairs, colonial rockers | swings, hammocks, ship's deck (steamer) recliners | director's chairs, patio chairs, wood stools and side tables; folding metal chairs; French park chairs, benches, and bistro tables; colonial hutches | wicker storage hampers, wicker or cane chairs, wicker chaises | carved, colonial-style poster beds, artist-painted headboards

WINDOW TREATMENTS plantation shutters with movable blades, hurricane shutters for inside use | linen Roman shades | white sheers | bamboo and wood beaded curtains | lace curtains, wide-blade wood blinds

SOFT FURNISHINGS mosquito net bed canopies | door drapes | white cotton and linen sheets and bedcovers, colorful accent prints on upholstery fabrics and toss pillows | colorful cotton dish towels | woven straw rugs

TABLETOP FURNISHINGS white or bright-colored china, plastic summer tableware | large trays, glass or plastic pitchers, chargers | enamelware flower vases, tubs, and buckets | woven place mats | black place mats

LIGHTING sunlight through shutter blades | metal or glass garden lanterns/candles | outdoor torches, electric light strings with colorful paper shades | table lamps with split cane shades | beaded chandeliers

FREE-FORM PATTERNS | SHELL MOTIFS | ANIMAL PRINTS | TIE-DYED FABRICS

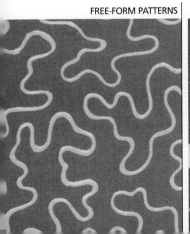
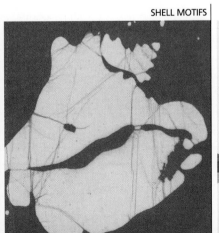

WRITING

ARITHMETIC.

56

Schoolhouse

KEYS TO THE STYLE

ESTABLISH a classroom palette at home. This decorating formula is a fun and practical style for families with children, making home and school transitions more comfortable. It's also an easy style to emulate because you already know how it goes together: Walls carry quiet blues and creams intended to calm; durable materials cover the floors, and big windows remain undecorated except for shades or blinds that roll up and down for privacy and light control.

INCORPORATE education paraphernalia, such as maps, blackboards, and measuring and communication devices, into the background to give this style its identity.

ORGANIZE rooms with furniture pieces that respond to active, busy lives. Invite library tables, locker room benches, desks, stackable chairs, vinyl lounge chairs, and twin-size dormitory beds into your home. Line walls with bookcases and carpet reading corners to muffle sound.

FILE away supplies in well-organized storage—some under covers and behind doors, others left out in the open for inspiration or practical use. Choose storage pieces that resemble items used in schools, such as lockers, bins, stackable crates, boxes, open shelves, hooks, filing cabinets, magazine files, and bookends.

PLAY at decorating. Arrange books to showcase their bindings. Line up neat magazine files of family photos, journals, scrapbooks, and mementos. Vary arrangements of items vertically and horizontally so shelves have an interesting rhythm. Play black against white with black school chairs in a white room or a white sofa against a blackboard wall. Stand a single flower bloom or two in a tall pot and place it in a space where it gets focal-point status. Create decoration from useful items.

A VERTICAL SWATH OF BLACKBOARD PAINT QUICKLY MAKES AN ARCHITECTURAL FOCAL POINT IN A FEATURELESS LIVING ROOM. AFTER THE PAINT DRIES, STROKE THE ENTIRE SURFACE WITH THE SIDE OF A CHALK STICK, COVERING IT COMPLETELY. WIPE AWAY MOST OF THE CHALK WITH A SOFT RAG TO LEAVE BEHIND A CHALKY, RAG-ROLLED EFFECT.

Living

Everything you need to know about decorating schoolhouse style you learned by the time you were in third grade. Teacher's pet or not, you have the tools and techniques you'll need for designing living spaces. The rest is in your shopping cart and the list of tips in this chapter.

Whether you prefer the idea of one-room schoolhouses of yesteryear or today's techno classrooms with flexible walls, computer cubicles, and intercoms, draw on your own experience to decorate with schoolhouse style. If old-time lunch pail shelves, a floor-standing water fountain, and coats hung on wall hooks inspire your schoolhouse look, you'll find what you need in the aisles of mass-market stores. If you want a modern schoolhouse look with high-gloss plastics and stainless-steel contemporary furniture, you'll find those items available too. For either approach the color palettes are the same.

Color walls with eggshell-finish latex paints for easy cleanup and for surfaces that wear better than those finished in flat paints. Simulate paneled walls with molding strips and paint subflooring or wood-planked floors with gray or white deck paint (white paint visually lifts the room higher than gray). On a wall or two, introduce chalkboard paint on a vertical panel, a pair of doors, or an entire wall that will hold a display of storage pieces. Shop for large-scale maps (check the yellow pages for local specialty stores that carry them) and use pushpins or vinyl wallpaper paste to hang them on walls as art.

A GOOD RULE: DECORATE WITH PAIRS TO GIVE A ROOM INSTANT ORDER, STABILITY, AND COMFORT.

Fit family meals into busy schedules with an attractive table, tasty food, and lots of adaptability.

A ROLLING CART ORGANIZES A LIBRARY OF COOKBOOKS. BE SURE CASTERS ARE STURDY ENOUGH TO BEAR THE WEIGHT (LOOK FOR WEIGHT RECOMMENDATIONS ON PACKAGING).

Use organizational items as design elements in eating zones. Open storage (hooks, shelves, and wall-hung racks) keeps attractive prime pieces within reach. A restaurant serving stand and black tray performs as an extra work surface or side table but folds away into a narrow slot when not in use. A school slate becomes a personalized place mat when you write a name on it. A handsome work island on wheels serves as a breakfast bar.

In the morning eat breakfast in the kitchen and pack lunches in canvas backpacks (store them on handy wall hooks *opposite* when they're not in use). Enjoy evening meals for two at a library table in the living room or, if everyone in the house comes home for dinner, celebrate with a meal at a long, cafeteria-style table. Sit on long benches or unstack the stackable chairs to seat everyone.

When preparing meals, move the cookbooks and recipe cards from one food prep area to another on a rolling cart *left*. Wrought-iron braces on the sides and back of the shelves keep items from falling off. Look for a cart with a top surface at a convenient waist height to make reading recipes easy. Then add a portable cookbook holder. Store recipe cards in galvanized tins and lunch boxes.

taste

drink

smell

2 1

3

time to go

A READY-TO-ASSEMBLE LAMINATE TABLE COMES HOME FROM A DECORATING
SUPERMARKET TO EXTEND THE USEFULNESS OF A FOCAL-POINT
CHALKBOARD/STORAGE WALL. SOMETIMES IT'S AN OFFICE DESK. AT OTHER
TIMES IT'S A DINING TABLE OR THE HUB OF A FAMILY CONFERENCE.

Dining.

SMALL BEDROOMS REQUIRE SIMPLE BED MAKING PROCEDURES AND COMPACT STORAGE.
BEDDING WITH A LARGE-SCALE GEOMETRIC PRINT MAKES A ROOM LOOK BIGGER. A GARAGE
LOCKER BECOMES A CLOSET AND A BIN-STYLE STORAGE UNIT DOUBLES AS A NIGHTSTAND.

Sleeping

Kick back in sleeping spaces that combine work, play, and rest—schoolhouse-style bedrooms are multitasking affairs. Furniture on wheels creates flexibility and a sense that rooms are works-in-progress open to change, growth, and fresh, new ideas.

Cool tones, especially those with deeper registers, create restful bedrooms. Select wall colors from your palette of greens, grays, and blues—any one of them will work to make zones for rejuvenation. Paint walls with flat latex paint. Tack a laminated map of the sky to the wall with pushpins for the sake of art and science. In a large bedroom shared by two or more, divide sleeping spaces with fabric walls that push back during the day.

When selecting bedding from discount or mass-market bed-and-bath store aisles, go for no-nonsense motifs, such as utilitarian stripes, squares, and plaids, that retain their crispness after many wash-and-dry cycles.

Shop for storage, storage, storage. When searching store aisles for good solutions, think beyond the usual bedroom storage pieces and matching chests. As you push the shopping cart down the aisles, remember school storage, such as lockers, open shelves, bins, crates, coat racks, hooks, and wire baskets, and see if you can find similar items to bring this practical look home.

AS THE GLOBE TURNS, SO DO WORK CENTERS. FOR OTHER ACTIVITIES, THESE COMPUTER DESKS ROLL TO THE SIDE.

Paperback Baskets ▲

MAKE THE MOST OF BOOKSHELF HEIGHTS AND
DEPTHS. PAPERBACKS ARE OFTEN SHORTER THAN
HARDCOVER BOOKS, LEAVING WASTED STORAGE
SPACE ON SHELVES. STOW THEM SIDEWAYS IN
ATTRACTIVE WIRE BASKETS THAT PULL OUT.

Door Art ▲

DESIGNATE "WALLS" TO WRITE ON WITH BLACKBOARD DOORS.
PREVENT THE GHOST EFFECT OF FIRST WORDS WRITTEN ON A NEWLY
PAINTED SURFACE BY USING THE SIDE OF A CHALK STICK TO COVER
THE BOARD WITH CHALK, THEN WIPE AWAY WITH A SOFT RAG.

Junk Chic ▲

BUY NEW ITEMS THAT IMITATE OLD ONES—THESE NEW
PLANTER BOXES ARE COPIES OF ANTIQUES. LINE
PLANTER BOXES WITH BOOKS SO YOU CAN MOVE
THEM FROM READING CORNER TO READING CORNER
OR FROM ROOM TO ROOM.

Recess Receptacles ▲

HOUSE RECREATIONAL EQUIPMENT IN STACKABLE METAL BOXES, SOME
WITH CASTERS FOR ROLLING AROUND ROOMS, OTHERS WITHOUT
CASTERS FOR STATIONARY STORAGE. CHECK STORES THAT SPECIALIZE IN
STORAGE OR CRUISE THE HOME STORAGE AISLES OF DISCOUNT MARKETS.
SOMETIMES CASTERS MAY BE PURCHASED SEPARATELY.

Planning the Look

COLOR Recall the institutional greens and blues of classrooms—colors that calmed and quieted youthful energy—to establish a color palette. Or plan to use all the colors in the guide *above*. Use black for accents and focal-point walls and neutrals for remaining walls and large surfaces on furniture. Use blues and greens on fabrics in patterns *below*.

PATTERN Stick with the geometrics of military schools and dormitories. Brandish bold stripes and plaids on bedcoverings and kitchen towels. Scan store aisles for simple graphics on rugs, upholstery fabric, or pillow coverings. If you come across yardage in fabric stores that reminds you of art class, such as finger painting, tie-dye, or handprints, incorporate it into rooms on slipcovers and sofa pillows. Add metal storage pieces with grid patterns.

TEXTURE Be practical. Choose smooth, lacquered storage lockers and hardworking table surfaces that resist marring and scoring. Snuggle into armchairs and sofas covered with sweatshirt fabric, soft velour, or velveteen. Make winter beds with fuzzy flannel or stretchy jersey knits; make summer beds in cool, smooth cottons. Bring slick, laminated surfaces (posters, maps, and globes) and shiny plastics or powder-coated pieces into the mix.

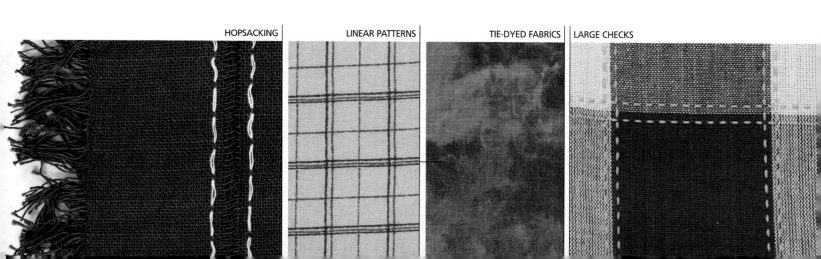

HOPSACKING   LINEAR PATTERNS   TIE-DYED FABRICS | LARGE CHECKS

What to Shop for

FURNITURE straight-lined sofa upholstered in washable white, gray, or green canvas or vinyl | plastic, wood, or wood/metal stackable chairs | benches used as seating or tables | plywood, metal, laminate, or wood tables, chairs, bed frames, nightstands, side tables, stools, armoires, storage units | utility shelving, wood or laminate wall-hung shelves, garage lockers | castered wood or plastic bins, boxes, carts, shelving units, chairs, and computer desks

WINDOW TREATMENTS roller shades | standard white sheers hung on stainless-steel rods | white wood, metal, or aluminum miniblinds | white cafe curtains | pleated shades or vertical blinds

SOFT FURNISHINGS white cotton or jersey-knit duvets, sheets, and pillowcases; striped corduroy or cotton bedcovers | terry cloth bath towels and bath mats | sweatshirt, rucksack, canvas, and velour fabrics for toss or floor-pillow coverings | cotton dish towels | sisal, coir, or cotton rugs

TABLETOP FURNISHINGS plain white china, bulk paper plates and napkins | stainless-steel flatware, pots, and pans | standard glasses and stemware

LIGHTING cable lighting | contemporary desk lights and floor-standing lamps | brushed-nickel desk lamps with white shades | track lights

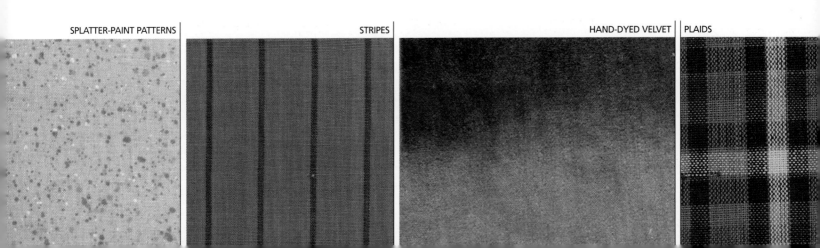

SPLATTER-PAINT PATTERNS | STRIPES | HAND-DYED VELVET | PLAIDS

Greenhouse

KEYS TO THE STYLE

THINK OUTSIDE IN. The reverse of isle style, which takes indoor elements outside (pages 44–55), this style brings the elements of the outdoors in. Floors and walls are clad in wood, clay tile, glass, metal, and stone or painted in earthy tans, creams, greens, and browns. Rugged, weathered textures give surfaces the desired look.

OPEN WINDOWS TO NATURE. Like a greenhouse that welcomes the sun through bare windows, greenhouse style leaves as many windows uncovered as possible. When privacy is needed, glass panes disappear behind lightweight window coverings of canvas, bamboo, paper, or wood.

BUY OUTDOOR FURNITURE. Porch and deck furnishings come inside. Begin with the three basics for any home—a bed, sofa, and dining table. Then fill out with smaller pieces. Import or mass-market stores are good places to find outdoor living furniture. Scan the aisles of garden centers for more choices.

NURTURE COMFORT. Use soft furnishings made from feel-good cottons, washable canvas, down, and woven sisal. Fill rooms with as much natural light as possible. When night falls, turn on floor and table lamps, keeping lights low for an intimate, cocoonlike mood. For artistic touches in the evening, place can lights or uplights behind large green plants to create dramatic leaf shadows on walls.

GROW MORE CREATIVE. Browse garden centers for items that inspire inventive ways to accessorize. A birdbath needn't be a birdbath if you think it makes a great base for a bedside table. Ditto for clay or metal garden urns. Or try these ideas: Collect smooth, flat field stones for tabletop decor; hang green plants across a window as a window treatment; assemble tabletop centerpieces from green-glazed terra-cotta pottery.

HALF LIVING AND HALF DINING ROOM, THIS SUNLIT SPACE WORKS HARD AT SERVING TWO PURPOSES. SPLIT DOWN THE MIDDLE, HALF OF THE ROOM CATERS TO DINING UNDER AN UMBRELLA TABLE. THE OTHER HALF SERVES AS A GATHERING PLACE FOR READING AND RELAXING.

Living

Two wonderful things about outdoor furnishings—flexibility and an immediate association with leisure-time activities—make designing rooms an easy pleasure. Greenhouse style encourages thinking outside the box and exploring fresh solutions for creating a home.

Solariums, porches, and added-on "green rooms" translate quickly into greenhouse style. Take cues from these rooms to expand the natural theme throughout the rest of your house. Paint walls with mint, celery, sage, or lime greens. Unify all woodwork in the house with a consistent color. Use all white for a light and airy look or wood-stained for a deeper, cozier feel. If you can, keep windows uncovered for the clear-pane look of a greenhouse full of plants. Add mullions to plain panes with home center inserts. Install French doors and bay or bow windows to gain more sunlight. Tile floors with clay or materials that have the look of stone.

Find furniture in stores that specialize in outdoor living. A pivotal piece of furniture in the sunny living/dining room *opposite* is a cushioned garden bench from an import store. Placed near the center of the room, it acts as a sofa on the living side of the room. The rectangular umbrella table, placed directly behind it, seats four for breakfast or lunch via two chairs and a picnic bench along the window side of the table. If six appear for dinner in the evening, the garden bench can be turned for seating along the other long side of the table.

Say yes to slipping a market umbrella in the slot of an umbrella table, even if it will never

shelter you from the sun or rain. It will bring a smile to the room and be a surprise for guests. Consider decorating with birdcages, storing books in a hobby store wheelbarrow, or hanging outdoor lighting inside. The finishing touch? Green plants, of course. Develop your green thumb to keep them thriving.

A PAIR OF WICKER WING CHAIRS CREATES A CALM OASIS FOR TWO IN A MANY-WINDOWED ROOM. ▲

Every meal's a picnic, minus the ants, when you venture into greenhouse style. Begin with an inviting easy-care table.

Round, square, hexagonal, octagonal, or rectangular, the array of outdoor table sets available in store aisles organizes casual dining quickly. Round tables work well in small spaces because the table has no corners to avoid. Long picnic tables work well in rooms set aside especially for dining. Bench seating is particularly appealing to large families with small children who can easily seat themselves without pulling chairs across the floor. Position the table as close to a window as possible to benefit from natural light and warm sunshine.

When choosing a round table, remember that a 36-inch-diameter table seats two, a 40-inch-diameter table seats four, and a 56-inch-diameter table seats eight. If you prefer a rectangular table, one 60 inches long seats six, 72- to 84-inch-lengths seat eight, and a 96-inch-long table seats ten.

Other than changing the wall color, one of the quickest and easiest ways to green up a dining room is to bring in plants. The sunny window ledge in the dining space *opposite* is too narrow for comfortable seating but makes an ideal place for potted plants in a variety of shapes and sizes. Garden store terra-cotta pots and saucers make handy centerpieces.

▲ STACKED AND LAYERED EARTHENWARE POTS FROM THE GARDEN STORE HOLD FRUITS, NUTS, AND NONFOOD ITEMS.

ONCE COLD AND EMPTY, THIS WHITE ROOM BECOMES HUMANIZED WITH TEXTURE—A SISAL RUG, COTTON TABLE COVERINGS, GREEN PLANTS, AND A BAMBOO VALANCE THAT HIDES METAL BLINDS.

Dining

A FENCE SECTION FROM A HOME CENTER TURNS INTO A RUSTIC HEADBOARD WHEN THE WIDTH IS CUT 6 TO 8 INCHES WIDER THAN A MATTRESS/BOX SPRING AND THE BOTTOM IS CUT SO THE HEIGHT OF THE HEADBOARD IS 4½ FEET.

Sleeping

Green bedrooms nurture and comfort.
They bring balance and tranquility to your
nocturnal dreams.

▼ CUT AWNING CANVAS, PURCHASED AT A FABRIC STORE, INTO A
ROLLER SHADE, PILLOW COVERS, AND A LAWN CHAIR SEAT. YOU'LL
FIND SHADE KITS AND PATTERNS AT THE FABRIC STORE TOO.

Different colors affect your mood in different ways. Green is known for its tranquilizing powers, suiting greenhouse-style sleepers who love the soothing colors and grounding effect of green grass and trees. If this style appeals to you, paint your bedroom walls one of the greens shown on pages 78–79. Then lie down on a bed of leaves with a fluffy duvet covered in leaf-patterned fabric.

You'll need to replace the mattress on your bed every five to ten years. The right mattress supports you so you can turn easily with your hips and shoulders gently cradled. Firm does not always mean better; it comes down to personal preference and body shape. A good mattress supports your spine and has a bit of give at the pressure points, where your body sinks deeper into the mattress. When buying a mattress, check labels to see how it's constructed. The most common type is innerspring, which is made of tempered spring coils covered with layers of padding and upholstery. Compare the number of coils and their construction, the number of padding layers and their material, and special features. The higher the number of coils, the better the bed will wear. A guideline is 300 coils for a double, 375 for a queen, and 450 to 600 for a king, each side topped with several layers of upholstery, one or more layers of foam, and a quilted pillow top.

Details make a difference

Side Table ▲

BUY A GARDEN CENTER URN FOR A TABLE BASE. FILL IT WITH SAND FOR STABILITY AND TOP IT OFF WITH A ROUND PIECE OF ¾-INCH-THICK GLASS (PURCHASE ONE THAT IS 5 TO 7 INCHES WIDER THAN THE DIAMETER OF THE URN).

Chandelier ▲

TO CREATE A FANCIFUL LIGHTING FIXTURE LIKE THIS WROUGHT-IRON CANDLEHOLDER, COMBINE GREEN-GLASS LANTERNS WITH HANGING CHAINS AND A DECORATIVE GARDEN ORNAMENT. THE KEY TO SUCCESSFUL COMBINING IS CHOOSING ITEMS WITH MATERIALS AND COLORS IN COMMON.

Leaf Motif ▲

DINE ON LEAVES AND OTHER GOODIES FROM
THE NATURAL WORLD. FOR EXAMPLE, USE A
LONG GREEN WOVEN RUG WITH INVITING
TEXTURES AND VARIED COLORS AS A TABLE
RUNNER. FRAME LEAF-PATTERNED CHINA WITH
GREEN METAL CHARGERS AND DECORATE THE
CENTER OF THE TABLE WITH FRAGILE FERNS IN
TERRA-COTTA POTS.

Leaf Pillows ▲

FOR PADDING OUTDOOR BENCHES, BUY DISCONTINUED UPHOLSTERY
SAMPLES, UPHOLSTERY CORDING, FIBERFILL, AND COORDINATING FABRICS
(FOR PILLOW BACKS AND CORDING COVERS). EDGE THE SAMPLE SQUARES
WITH COVERED PIPING. WITH RIGHT SIDES FACING, SEW EACH PILLOW BACK
TO A FRONT ALONG RAW EDGES, LEAVING AN OPENING FOR TURNING.
TURN RIGHT SIDE OUT, STUFF WITH FIBERFILL, AND HAND-SEW CLOSED.

Planning the Look

COLOR Inspiration for decorating is all around you—through any window in your house, at a public botanical garden, or on a walk in the woods. For a fun way to begin a decorating scheme, gather natural elements that appeal to you. Unless they are flowers or fruit, most natural bits and pieces—nuts, woods, stones, leaves, and twigs—fall in the green and brown ranges of color. Pull together several items as your design inspiration and display them in a bowl while you plan. Whole schemes can develop from such simple beginnings.

PATTERN The most obvious pattern choices for soft furnishings, wallcoverings, or tableware come from manufacturers' interpretations of nature's leaves, vines, stones, and wood grains. Scan store aisles for large- and small-scale pattern mixes. Remember to balance two or three pictorial patterns with geometrics, such as plaids or checks.

TEXTURE Greenhouse style is also about texture, such as the smoothness of windowpanes where raindrops slide; the rough weaves of burlap, canvas, or sisal, and the fine ones of cotton; the dull, pitted surfaces of terra-cotta and stone; slick steel; rough sisal; soft leaves; and velvety flower petals. Balance pattern choices with plain-colored items that have interesting surfaces.

ROUGH-WEAVE FABRICS

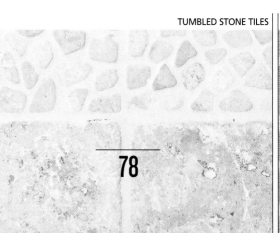

TUMBLED STONE TILES

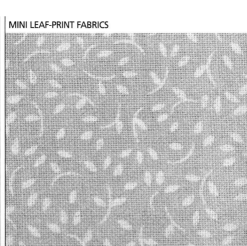

MINI LEAF-PRINT FABRICS

What to Shop for

FURNITURE wooden or metal garden benches with backs, arms, and padded seats | lumberyard fence sections for headboards | folding lawn chairs, outdoor bar and patio table sets | bamboo, wicker, teak, or wrought-iron chairs, tables, trunks, wardrobes, and shelving | urn or birdbath side tables | rolling barbecue carts for chair or tableside service | picnic tables, benches

WINDOW TREATMENTS striped roller shades | grommeted cotton canvas draperies | bamboo valances over roll-up blinds | white sheers | leaf-print cafe curtains hung on wood poles | wood or rice paper blinds

SOFT FURNISHINGS white canvas market umbrellas, table coverings, and seat cushions; chenille throws | cotton, canvas, and denim fabrics in plaids and checks; leaf-patterned fabrics for toss pillows, upholstery cushions, or bed linens | sisal, bamboo, or coir area rugs; cotton woven rag rugs

TABLETOP FURNISHINGS terra-cotta, leaf-motif china, or plain flower-colored dishes; metal chargers | stainless-steel flatware, pots, pans, and chargers | green-glass drinking glasses, stemware | green plants in terra-cotta pots

LIGHTING bamboo-pole floor lamps | leaf-motif paper, wicker, or handmade paper shades on floor and table lamps | steel pendant lamps

HAND-DYED FABRICS | CHECKS AND PLAIDS | LARGE LEAF PATTERNS | FREE-FORM VINE DESIGNS

Soft Modern

KEYS TO THE STYLE

■**PASTEL BACKDROPS.** This style is especially suited to contemporary, newly built suburban homes. Light wood, white or neutral floors, carpets, and architectural trims slip into the background to play a supporting role in decorating. Understated walls wear a soft array of powder puff pastels that hush the rooms.

■**SHEER WINDOW TREATMENTS.** Curtains emphasize surface textures and barely-visible patterns, inviting the sunlight to play through them with bright shafts of light and shifting shadows.

■**ROUNDED FURNITURE SHAPES.** These pieces put a curve on the stiff, straight-lined concept of modern furniture design. Choose sofas, chairs, tables, storage pieces, and beds with steel, chrome, or light wood frames that keep rooms pale and lustrous. For upholstery fabrics go neutral with white canvas, soft gray or tan leather, or bold, neutral stripes. Wrought-iron or light-painted wood chairs are another option.

■**VARIED TEXTURES.** Most decorating schemes depend on color for surface decoration. Soft modern counts on texture to do the job. Play opposing textures off each other: Place soft velvet opposite bumpy, beaded quilting on sofa pillows. Stack tucked, patchwork, or tufted pillows on a smooth bamboo floor. Lay sleek satins near feathery fringes or shiny metallic-looking cushions on a crocheted lamb's wool throw.

■**LIGHT AND SHINE.** Put a sheen on every room with natural light, lamps, and utilitarian or decorative objects. The final beauty of soft-modern style lies in the combination of the matte and shiny finishes you fold into the pale, textural palette.

DISCRIMINATING EYES SEE THE DELICATE STRIPES PAINTED IN THIS ROOM. TO CREATE THE MATTE-SHINY EFFECT, PAINT WALLS FLAT YELLOW, MASK OFF 18-INCH-WIDE STRIPES, AND BRUSH EVERY OTHER STRIPE WITH CLEAR POLYURETHANE. ▼

Living

Choose one pastel background color per room to showcase modern furnishings for living softly in a contemporary world. Pale yellow, the color of intellect and thought, promotes sunny feelings and a sense of well-being. Light blue, the color of calm, is especially suited to bedrooms. Soft green, health and vigor, balances moods while pink or peach (white versions of red or orange) make a room feel smaller, cozier, and energized.

Build a structure for living with white and/or neutral-colored floors, doors, and window frames; light wood tables; and neutral seating pieces that have light wood or metal frames. Define the seating group with a large area rug with a modern design. Bring attention to the main seating piece with contrasting cushions, some plain and one with a focal-point surface.

Punch up the soft scheme with small accents of black (note the black line through the rug design and the black and white photographs on the mantel *opposite*). The dark gray laminate shelves and black-on-white book spines, *right,* add more accents on another wall in the room. Fill out open storage with a display of useful objects with appealing matte and shiny surfaces.

Light has the power to make color thrive, patinas shimmer, and an empty space come alive. Set up a dining table near a window *left* and *opposite*. Place green leafy plants, a potted tree, or a vase of flowers in front of the window to heighten the sense of nature indoors.

Use glass to reflect light and mirrors to multiply and energize it. Keep window treatments sheer, translucent, and casual to let in natural light. Sleek-looking blinds filter strong sun and provide privacy.

Borrow light from the next room by removing doors that separate adjoining spaces. In a small room with no natural illumination, create a small interior window to access light from a neighboring room.

Enhance the light-reflecting quality of glossy wood furniture by applying a paste wax periodically to keep the wood lustrous.

Balance light with color. When a room is cooled by a shady tree or a northern exposure, *opposite,* turn up the temperature with warm tones, such as peach, pink, or yellow. Balance the warm light from a southern exposure *left* with cool blue or green.

WINDOW FILM THAT FILTERS ULTRAVIOLET (UV) LIGHT PREVENTS WINDOW FABRICS FROM FADING.

A 1970S KITCHEN GETS A FACELIFT WITH A CRAFTY PALETTE OF MATERIALS AND TEXTURES. BAMBOO, A RECENT ADVANCEMENT IN TONGUE-AND-GROOVE FLOORING, IS AVAILABLE FOR DO-IT-YOURSELFERS. ▼

Dining

SEDUCTIVE FABRICS MEET FEATHERS AND FRINGES ON A BED FIT FOR HIGH DRAMA. SCARVES (CHECK FASHION SECTIONS OF STORES) TURN INTO CURTAINS AND CANOPIES WHEN SLIPPED OVER WINDOW TENSION RODS OR SLIM RODS HUNG FROM THE CEILING ON PLANT HOOKS. ▼

Sleeping

86

Get to know your pillows inside and out—soft modern sleep style depends on it. Desired not only for the feel of luxury and comfort, pillows carry a palette of surface patterns and textures that please and entertain the eye. Play them off against pale walls, glass, and metal accents.

Dressing the bed with an inviting mix of fabrics is key. Stay with pale colors but explore eccentric trims (costume feathers, beads, or fringes) and machine-stitched detailing. Shop for wily contrasts, combining shiny, matte, tucked, printed, beaded, and quilted fabrics in neutral tones. Or shop with a one-color plan, such as pale blues, pinks, or yellows.

When deciding what to lay your head on for the night, determine your favorite sleeping position. Soft pillows are for stomach sleepers and usually are all down. A medium pillow, for back sleepers, will be half down and half feather. A firm pillow, for side sleepers, will be about 90 percent feather.

Down pillows can cost $25 to more than $200. As with comforters, the price depends on the proportion of down to feathers in the filling. The more down, the more expensive the pillows.

Other options: Better polyester pillows are filled with hollow-core fibers coated with silicone. Foam rubber wears out sooner and doesn't conform as easily to your head. For allergy sufferers the antibacterial cotton-filled pillows offer some relief.

IN A LIVING SPACE, A TWIN-SIZE MATTRESS AND BOX SPRING MAKE AN INVITING DAYBED OR GUEST QUARTERS.

Details make a difference

House Jewelry

SLIP LARGE GROMMETED CURTAIN PANELS OVER A
SLIM ROD WITH TRANSPARENT FINIALS. BEAUTIFUL
HARDWARE, LIKE JEWELRY, PUTS THE FINISHING
TOUCH ON A ROOM.

Green Bouquet

ARRANGE A BOUQUET WITHOUT FLOWERS. CROSS LONG STRANDS OF
BEAR GRASS OVER EACH OTHER TO MAKE DRAMATIC CURVES ON A
COFFEE OR SIDE TABLE. ASK YOUR LOCAL FLORIST FOR BEAR GRASS.

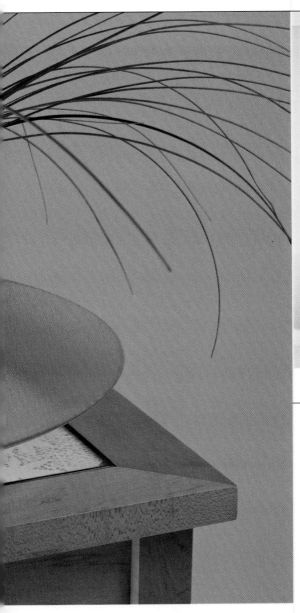

Soft Covers ▲

WHEN TITLES ON BOOKENDS JUMP OFF
SHELVES TOO GRAPHICALLY, SOFTEN THEM
WITH VELLUM BOOK COVERS. YOU'LL BE
ABLE TO READ THE TITLES, AND THE
BOOKCASES WILL GAIN THE SOFT
MODERN STYLE OF THE REST OF
THE ROOM.

Text Message ▲

SPLASH A BATH WITH LETTERING TO
SPELL OUT WHAT'S GOING ON. FIND
TOWEL BARS AND TOWELS THAT SAY
"WASH" AND "DRY" OR HANG SINGLE
LETTERS TO CREATE "BATH" OR "SPA."

Planning the Look

COLOR The soft modern palette is created from red, blue, yellow, and green. However, because these primary hues are diluted with white, they don't compete with each other or demand attention. You can successfully mix and match any and all colors when you collect them in their palest versions. Choose a blue, yellow, pink, or green theme for each room to enjoy subtle color changes as you move through the house.

PATTERN When choosing soft furnishings, look for modern curved lines and bands, rounded shapes, stripes, and uncomplicated geometrics. Scan store aisles for large, neutral-colored contemporary patterns on rugs, upholstery fabric, or pillow coverings. Use no more than one or two patterns in a room since you will count on texture to do most of the soft modern decorative work.

TEXTURE Create a visual feast of subtle textures that require an appreciative, discriminating eye. Combine the smooth sheen of metal with satin and silk. Play transparent glass against sunlight and garden greenery; combine sheers with feathers and fringes or pale, smooth woods with velvet and porcelain. Focus an entire room on a beaded cushion. On shelves, group slick glass, matte-finish ceramics, bound leather, and chrome. Buy neutral patchworks.

SOFT-PRINT FLANNELS   CRINKLE SATINS   CURVY PRINTS

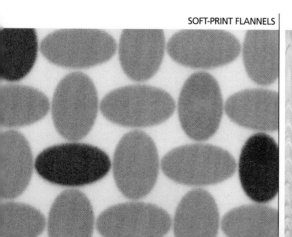

What to Shop for

FURNITURE straight-lined sofa upholstered in neutral-colored fabric, canvas, or leather   curved contemporary chairs with wood or metal frames   pale, light wood tables, dining chairs, chests of drawers, nightstands, and armoires   frosted glass tabletops on brushed nickel table frames   gray laminate shelving with brushed nickel frames   metal bed frames   nesting tables

WINDOW TREATMENTS vertical blinds (try narrow blades)   aluminum miniblinds   white sheer, voile, satin, silk, or cotton panels   fringed white scarves loosely hung on tension rods   velvet draperies   Roman shades

SOFT FURNISHINGS quilted satin duvets, charmeuse, silk, or satin bed linens   velvet, cotton, canvas, or leather upholstery fabrics   tucked, beaded, crinkled, embroidered, and patchwork moire, taffeta, and leather fabrics on sofa and floor cushions   sisal, hooked, or cotton-weave rugs

TABLETOP FURNISHINGS glass plates, bowls, cups, pitchers, stemware, and serving bowls   stainless-steel flatware, pots, pans, chargers   ceramic and glass vases   white porcelain or ceramic platters and trays   pale tablecloths

LIGHTING cable lighting   brushed nickel floor and table lamps with contemporary lines   glass sconces with metal hardware   track lights

QUILTED MOIRES   CORDED PATCHWORKS   GRAPHIC RUGS   SATIN CORDED FABRICS

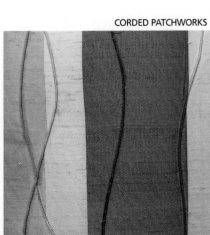

Salon Style

KEYS TO THE STYLE

■BUILD A BACKDROP. Create a dramatic setting for family and friends to inspire discussion and thought. Salon style fills walls from floor to ceiling with paintings, books, and travel souvenirs. Begin room designs with inspiring posters—for a small amount of money, you're off to a big start.

■CURTAINS UP. Salon style windows may be best when heavily draped, at least in rooms where art is the focus, darkness is desirable, and windows detract. However, in other rooms a lighter treatment may be in order.

■SPEAK WITH A FRENCH ACCENT. French furnishings are associated with salon style, which developed primarily in France where Impressionism provoked lively discussions. Never mind that nothing you have comes from France. It's the look that counts. Buy new curves—a half-round, or demilune table is classic French style, a Louis look-alike has royal influence, and cabriole legs whisper "français."

■FABRICATE. Swathe your home in layers of linens, velvets, faux furs, and luxury goods. Dressing your home with salon style is a bit like costuming a play or dressing up for a night on the town. Hidden beneath fringes, tassels, textures, and patterns, the bones of each room are colored in a limited palette that keeps this over-the-top decorating scheme under control.

■LIGHT LAMPS. If one characteristic of salon style stands out, it could be the element of creative lighting. While many styles in this book count on natural light for their moods, salon style depends on special effects lighting for intimacy and grace. Think of low lights on restaurant tables, lanterns on cobblestone streets, and stage lights at the Moulin Rouge. Note the use of lamps and curved shades on the following pages.

Living

A PAIR OF STATELY BOOKCASES HOUSES A LIBRARY OF LITERARY HEROES AND
CREATES A BACKDROP FOR LUXURIOUS LEATHER SEATING FROM AN IMPORT
STORE. ARTWORKS, ORIGINAL AND REPRODUCED, GIVE THE ROOM VITALITY.

Drink a toast to princely rooms at pauper prices. Thanks to mass-market stores, you can live in elegance and grace.

A PAIR OF HARLEQUIN-PATTERNED LAMPS AND A THEATER POSTER HUNG OVER ASIAN POTTERY ON A WROUGHT-IRON DEMILUNE TABLE PROVIDE A FORMAL ENTRANCE TO THIS ROOM. ▼

Inspired by Europe's 19th century salons where literary and artistic gatherings occurred in the stylish homes of prominent people, this style of the rich and famous can be yours today. All you need is a shopping cart and a creative exhibition of your decorating skills.

Begin with dark paneled walls or walls painted in a warm Lautrec yellow *right*. The idea is to create a deep cocoon of private space to gather family and friends. The faux paneling *opposite* is made by fastening a grid of dark-painted 1×3s over drywall painted in a lighter tone of the same color (this grid is based on the width and height of the bookcases for a unified look). Fasten posters in each rectangle of the grid between a pair of bookcases or display one or two paintings on easels as shown here. Arrange books in the shelves, placing travel souvenirs here and there among the titles.

For lively evenings of discussion, fill the living space with comfortable leather seating pieces or overstuffed, upholstered chairs. Purchase a two-seat sofa—usually only two people sit on a sofa. (Sitting three or four in a row on a long sofa feels stiff and formal, cutting down on social comfort.) A circle of five or six club chairs, an island of comfort for each person, invites the most relaxed camaraderie. Provide extra cushions and throws for easing back into the curves of chairs. Toss floor cushions on an area rug to extend seating and place round tea tables and trays for hors d'oeuvres and party fare in easy reach.

Design dining spaces as if you were meeting for espresso at a French cafe or dining out at a restaurant before attending the theater.

Never the star attraction of the day, dining salon style is part of a larger whole—a warm-up before a venue or the wrap-up after a ball game. Before, after—even during—an event, dining is a secondary pleasure to (or diversion from) life happening around you.

If salon style dining sounds like fast-food meals-on-wheels or tripping through restaurants on the run, remember that salon style dining is done with style and grace within the confines of an elegant home. Here are two old-world salon-style lessons:

Round tables promote intimate dining and a free flow of conversation around the table. Because there is no head of table, each diner is equal to the next. Because they have no corners to cause bruises, round tables are easy to walk around, especially in small spaces. They also can include more guests than a square table of similar size.

Table lamps take ordinary meals to a higher level of excitement. Set a main dining room table close enough to the side of a room to use a wall socket. Or use an umbrella table so the cord can travel through tablecloths (stitched with buttonholes at the center of the table) and under a rug to the side of the room. Another option: candle lamps with theatrical shades.

ACHIEVE A LOOK OF OLD-WORLD DINING WITH TOILE AND SATIN, WICKER AND WIRE, PORCELAIN AND GOLD.

A THEATER POSTER IS A BIG-BANG-FOR-THE-BUCK PURCHASE AT ANY MASS-MARKET STORE. PLACED ON AN EASEL AS A BACKDROP, IT HOSTS SMALL, BISTRO-SIZE END TABLES THAT SERVE AS A DINING SPACE WITHIN A LIVING ROOM. UPHOLSTERY PIECES OFFER COMFORTABLE SEATING FOR LINGERING OVER GOOD CONVERSATION AND DRINKS.

Dining

Sleeping

AN OVERSIZE MOULIN ROUGE POSTER WOWS THE EYES. THE BLACK FRAME OF THE BED ECHOES THE BLACK FRAME OF THE ARTIST'S WORK AND SATIN CHARMEUSE SHEETS ENCOURAGE QUALITY SLEEP.

Dressing a salon style bed is like costuming a play—drama is the key to decorating success.

Take your bedroom center stage with larger-than-life furnishings and striking fabrics that make you feel like a colorful character in a theatrical production.

Paint a soft backdrop in pale colors so furnishings get the starring role in the space. Screen windows with sheer panels. Unlike room-darkening velvet theater curtains, these allow the sun to light your stage by day.

Make the bed the focal point. Invest in a good mattress and box spring and scout up a bed frame with star quality. Position the bed so the headboard faces the doorway. (It's *feng shui* to be able to view the door from your bed.) If you need more storage than your closet allows, buy bins on wheels to roll under the bed. Another storage option: travel trunks.

"Prop" the room using pieces that delight your sensibilities and weave fragments of your personality into the bedroom story. For old-world style with French appeal, buy bedside chests with curved fronts and cabriole legs, wicker picture frames with wrought-iron embellishments, and tall, thin bedside lamps with out-turned shades. A coatrack with scrolled hooks displays favorite accessories, and beaded pillows dress up boudoir chairs.

BIG MIRRORS ON WARDROBE DOORS EXPAND THE SPACE AND REFLECT FURNISHINGS, DOUBLING THEIR IMPACT. ▲

Details make a difference

Private Secretary ▲

CORNER A DESK FOR THE SAKE OF WRITING
BEAUTIFUL THANK-YOU NOTES AND SENDING OUT
INVITATIONS TO PARTIES OR RESPONDING TO THOSE
WHO INVITED YOU TO THEIRS. CHOOSE HANDMADE
PAPERS WITH LOVELY-TO-THE-TOUCH SURFACES.

Secret Boxes ▲

HIDE CLUTTER AND TREASURES AWAY WITH STYLISH STORAGE. THE
RIGHT STUFF? A LEOPARD-PRINT LIDDED STOOL (WHO KNEW?), A GOLD-
GILT BOX, AND A WICKER CASE WITH A CURVED WOOD BASE.

Luxury Layers ▲

MORE IS BETTER. INEXPENSIVE COTTON COORDINATED SETS OF DECORATOR TABLE COVERINGS FROM STORE AISLES PRODUCE A LOT OF LOOK FOR LESS. HERE A ROUND PAISLEY UNDERSKIRT IS TOPPED WITH A LAYER OF RED AND CREAM STRIPES. NO ONE IMAGINES THE BARE-BONES CHIPBOARD TABLE BENEATH IT ALL.

Gilded Louis ▲

LOUIS, THAT RASCAL KING, FILLED ROOMS WITH CURVACEOUS CHAIRS, FLUFFY WIGS, AND DANGEROUS LIAISONS. TURN HEADS IN YOUR PALACE WITH A GILDED REPRODUCTION CHAIR OR TWO. TO DECORATE REMOVE THE SEATS AND SPRAY THE BODY OF THE CHAIR WITH AN AEROSOL CAN OF GOLD PAINT. THEY'LL NEVER BELIEVE YOU DID IT YOURSELF!

| RENOIR RED | | WILDE ROSE | GAUGUIN | | LAUTREC YELLOW | VAN GOGH |

Planning the Look

COLOR Gather a warm palette of golds, peaches, reds, and browns with paint store chips, home center wood-stain samples, and snippets of plain-colored fabrics. Keep your choices close in value with about the same lightness and darkness. Because of their equal values and neighborliness on the color wheel, you can use these colors successfully in whatever varying amounts you choose. Plan to use black in small amounts on frames, table legs, and lamp bases.

PATTERN Practice salon style patterning by snipping patterns from magazine pictures and adding them to your color box. Look for harlequin prints, curved scrollwork, impressionistic posters, paisleys, stripes, and toiles. Collect fabric store samples of luxury fabrics (some stores offer samples of decorator fabrics). In window-shopping mode, tour the aisles of many stores before making purchases. If a purchase doesn't "work" (fit, look good, match) when you get it home, take advantage of the store's return policy.

TEXTURE Balance your color and pattern plans with texture—salon style loves all three with equal measure. Fuzzy faux furs, rough wicker weaves, smooth wrought iron or glass, sumptuous leather, and luxurious velvets or silks bring drama and elegance home.

| VARIEGATED STRIPES | | BOLD STRIPES | SCROLL PATTERNS |

What to Shop for

FURNITURE leather or fabric upholstered sofas and chairs with rounded, low-profile Euro-inspired lines | round and half-round (demilune) tables | wrought-iron bed frames, table bases, coatracks, easels, and dressing room screens | wood bistro, bentwood, or Louis-style dining chairs | wood bookcases, curved chests of drawers, writing desks | dark wicker chests, screens, and serving carts on wheels | decorator and glass-topped tables

WINDOW TREATMENTS dark velvet "stage-curtain" panels with tab tops or pleated headings | pastel sheers | silk, satin, or charmeuse floor-to-ceiling panels with tasseled or swagged valances | beaded valances

SOFT FURNISHINGS pastel satin, charmeuse, silk, or Egyptian cotton sheets, pillowcases, tablecloths, and napkins | patterned bath towels and bath mats | faux fur, velvet, and tufted toss-pillow coverings | sisal, coir, or cotton rugs

TABLETOP FURNISHINGS white porcelain or silver-plate espresso cups, plates, and bowls | stainless-steel or gold-edged flatware, stemware, and chargers | faceted glassware | votive candles, tealights, crystal candleholders

LIGHTING candles, crystal chandeliers | floor and table lamps with curved shades | wrought-iron or metal candle chandeliers | uplights

TUFTED TEXTURES | PAISLEY PRINTS | FAUX FUR | EMBROIDERY

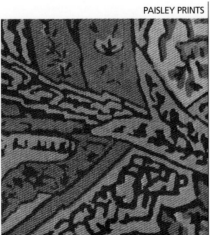
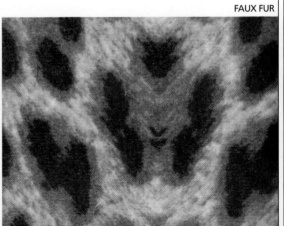

Bollywood

KEYS TO THE STYLE

■ **DECORATE WITH FLAMBOYANCE.**
Explore the exuberance of Bollywood,
India's glittery version of Hollywood
located in Bombay. The movie
industry's divas and darlings dress in
shimmering costumes exaggerated for
maximum effect. Likewise Bollywood
homes are temples to saturated color,
rich pattern, and cultural assimilation.

■ **IMAGINE A BACKDROP.** Think of
your living spaces as Bollywood
theater, where life plays out for real.
Design a stunning set with hot-color
walls, fretwork panels, and pointed
arches. Layer floors with elaborate
carpets. Dress windows with
diaphanous curtains, stained glass,
louvers, slats, and shutters.

■ **SET THE SCENE.** Cultivate India's
assimilation of cultures by selecting
"Made-in-India" tables, chairs, and
handcrafted storage pieces. Include
British Colonial camelback sofas and
plantation pieces as well as tiled and
painted pieces that exhibit Islamic
decorative influences.

■ **DRAMATIZE WITH FABRIC.** Spread
flower-strewn carpets on the floors.
Drape lotus-inspired shawls and
embroidered mirrorwork throws over
beds and sofas. Veil tabletops with
delicate paisleys and lacy crochet.
Cascade saffron velvets and silky
brocades down staircase walls.
Combine diversities, such as
patchwork bed linens from the
villages of Rajasthan, south Indian
hand-loomed checked weaves,
kantha embroidery from West Bengal,
and gossamer sari silks from Gujarat.

■ **ADD SPECIAL EFFECTS.** As if
dramatic textiles aren't enough,
accelerate the color effects of the
fabric festival with mood-heightening
lamps and lights. Tree-of-life forged
iron candelabras for tables and floors
put a gleam on the metallics in a
room. Candlelights bless the space
with their own kind of atmosphere,
and electrical lights and lanterns make
it possible to read the fine print.

A SWING CHAIR, CUT FROM A SOLID-CORE DOOR, HANGS FROM THE CEILING BY CHAINS AND LARGE SCREW EYES. LIKE A HAMMOCK WITH LAZY, GENTLE MOVEMENTS, IT OFFERS BLISSFUL SEATING. FOR MORE COMFORT PAD THE SWING WITH A THICK FOAM CUSHION COVERED WITH AN EMBROIDERED THROW.

Living

See your living space as a place where mind and body revive. Here you drink in color, absorb the patterns, and relax amidst billowing layers of soft fabrics. Such rooms are all about pleasing your senses, celebrating beauty, and creating special moods and effects.

Paint plain walls with "architecture" that's part foreign, part domestic. Rough-plaster Indian walls are often painted with bright colors that accent arches and niches or create arched shapes on brick walls. At home get a similar effect by painting a Bollywood arch on a focal-point wall, such as this one *opposite*.

First paint the entire wall with the main color. For the arch use an arched import store mirror, frame, or cabinet door as inspiration. Cut a length of butcher paper the width of the wall; fold it in half crosswise. Draw half (one side) of the arch shape onto the paper, cut on the line through the two layers of paper, and open the length of paper out to reveal the complete arch. Fasten the top half of the paper to the wall temporarily with painter's tape, adjusting it until the arch is in the desired position. Draw the arch line on the wall with a pencil; toss the paper. Use painter's tape to mask off the line below the arch line (follow curves closely with small strips for a precise line). Paint the arch portion above the tape in a contrasting color; remove the tape.

Furnish the room with a combination of western-style seating and traditional Indian hardwood tables, chairs, and lighting fixtures.

PAIRING STRONG COMPLEMENTARIES, SUCH AS PURPLE AND YELLOW, BRINGS POWERFUL VIBES TO A SITTING ROOM.

If spicy fabrics and glittering textures whet your appetite for decorating, give Bollywood dining style a whirl.

Dazzle a dining room with a wainscot that follows the architecture of windows, coloring the lower section with a darker tone than the one above it. The dining room *opposite* is an example. A good height for a wainscot on an 8-foot-high wall is about 70 inches. For a focal point on a plain wall, assemble a *trompe l'oeil* window with wood shutters, mirror tile, and "wagon wheel" brackets from the lumberyard. Follow the lines of the arch when painting the backdrop, framing it with 2-inch margins.

Stitch together two sarongs (beach wraps from import stores) to make a rich and colorful table covering *opposite*. Look for intensely colored pieces with gold or silver metallic borders at the hems and single motifs spaced evenly over the upper sections. Another option: two white crinkle-cotton sarongs with cutwork lace borders at the hem provide a white table covering to contrast with and showcase the tableware you put on top of it.

Serve meals accompanied by elaborate bowls of gold- or silver-trimmed glass balls (imported Christmas ornaments are good finds). Arrange glass lanterns for sparkle on kiln dried, seasoned Indian hardwood buffets, sideboards, or plantation-style serving trays. Hang electrical mesh lanterns overhead for general or ambient lighting.

MIX COMPLEMENTARY HUES OF SIMILAR TONES WITH METALLICS TO BRING BOLLYWOOD COLORS TO THE TABLE.

THE DAZZLING EFFECT OF PANELS OF METALLIC FABRIC IS DOUBLED BY THEIR REFLECTION IN THE MIRROR TILE OF THE *TROMPE L'OEIL* WINDOW ON THE OPPOSITE WALL.

Dining ▲

THIS BOUDOIR'S HEADY BLEND OF SAFFRON, SHOCKING PINKS, PURPLES, AND REDS IS
COOLED AND REFRESHED WITH STRONG ACCENTS OF WHITE, SILVER, AND CREAM.

Sleeping

Star in your own bedroom story with sizzling-hot walls, sumptuous fabrics, and intricately handcrafted metallics.

A CHANNEL-STITCH QUILT WITH SINGLE MOTIFS AND A FLORAL BORDER TYPIFIES TRADITIONAL PATTERNS INTERPRETED IN MODERN, SCREEN-PRINTED FABRICS. THIS ECLECTIC MIX OF IMPORT STORE PIECES SHOWS INDIA'S UNIQUE BLEND OF ISLAMIC, BRITISH COLONIAL, AND NATIVE CULTURAL STYLING.

Set the stage for a stunning sleep space by painting the walls lipstick pink. Then paint the floor pure white to cool the room and reflect the strong color—a little shocking pink goes a long way.

To furnish the space, go with a consistent dark wood theme *left* or an all-white furniture scheme *opposite* rather than mixing the two. Block out the room with a sleeping platform (bed frame with headboard) or a room-within-a-room effect with a colonial-style poster bed. Add bedside tables made from low-to-the-ground divan chairs, folding tray tables, carved or handpainted wood trunks, or small wood-carved cabinets.

For Bollywood-style luxury add a low tea table with floor cushions set on a woven dhurrie or chindi rug. Buy a floor screen with forged ironwork panels, brass inserts, or intricate wood-carved "beehive" patterns. If you find the right pieces of furniture in dark wood and you want a white furniture scheme, paint them white. First apply a coat of stain-preventing paint (ask for a brand at your paint store counter). Then apply two coats of satin finish white latex paint.

Complete the diva space with silky fringed scarves looped over canopy rails, dress-up gowns hung from folding screens, and beaded pillows arranged over an Indian cotton bedspread. Knot long, dramatic swaths of colorful voiles or metallic polyesters found at the fabric store (check the bridal section) and float them loosely over curtain rods.

Details make a difference

Sense Pleasers ▲

TAKE TIME TO APPRECIATE THE FINER THINGS—A VELVETY ROSE WITH A FLORAL SCENT, A BOOK PRINTED IN SANSKRIT, AND MINIATURE FLOWERS ON A SILKEN PILLOW. PLAY MUSIC FOR THE EARS AND BURN INCENSE FOR THE RITUAL OF IT. SIP GINGER TEA.

Metallic Block Prints and Shiny Beads ▲

GO FOR THE GOLD. LAYER INDIAN TEXTILES ON A MADDER RED SOFA IN A SHOWCASE OF PATTERN. YOU'LL FIND BEAD-TRIMMED BLOCK PRINTS ON SHAWLS, CUSHIONS, AND CANDLES IN IMPORT STORES NEAR YOU.

Scarf Dance ▲

WITH TWO LARGE SILVER CLIPS FROM AN OFFICE SUPPLY STORE, FASHION A DRAMATIC FLOURISH AT YOUR WINDOW. FIRST MOUNT A 36-INCH LENGTH OF THREADED ROD FROM A HARDWARE STORE AS A CURTAIN ROD; BUY THREADED ROD NUTS AND SCREW THEM ONTO THE ENDS OF THE RODS FOR FINIALS. SLIDE A SHEER PRIVACY PANEL ONTO THE ROD. THEN, WITH THE SILVER CLIPS, FASTEN THE CORNERS OF ONE END OF A SARI SCARF ONTO THE ROD OVER THE FIRST PANEL, LEAVING A LOOSE, STYLISH CURVE AT THE CENTER.

Hanging Lanterns ▲

LIGHT HANGING CANDLES FOR MAGICAL MOODS. YOU'LL FIND DOZENS OF VOTIVE-HOLDING CHOICES IN IMPORT STORES. SOME HAVE WIRES FOR SWINGING FROM PLANT HOOKS FASTENED TO THE CEILING. OTHERS HANG FROM METAL TABLETOP OR FLOOR STANDS FITTED WITH HOOKS FOR HANGING BEADED GLASS VOTIVE CUPS.

Planning the Look

▼

COLOR Bollywood colors are strongly saturated hues associated with gems—topaz, sapphire, ruby, and emerald—or spices—saffron, cayenne, and ginger. For color success combine complementaries (reds with greens, purples with yellows, blues with oranges) with equal tonal values. Or group several from the same color family (cool blues/greens or hot pinks/reds) in similar tones. Plan to balance the bright colors with refreshing whites and accents of silver and gold.

PATTERN Plant and animal patterns—mango leaves, lotus, garlands of flowers, parrots, elephants, mythical birds, and trees of life—are typical of India's pattern history. Take a field trip through a world-market import store where you'll find traditional Indian handcrafts created for modern day use. Read labels and tags (look for "Made in India") to learn about India's specialized paisleys and elaborate geometrics. Buy a few pieces to get started.

TEXTURE Bollywood's tapestry of textures is rich with ornamentation and embellishment. While you're checking patterns in import stores, put your hands on India's gossamer cottons, silky brocades, metal cutwork, iron forgeries, carved hardwoods, and gold embroideries. Bring home a shiny mirrorwork, a soft cotton rug, or a smoothly painted tile.

GOLD BLOCK PRINTS

FLOWER PATTERNS | FLOATING PAISLEY MOTIFS

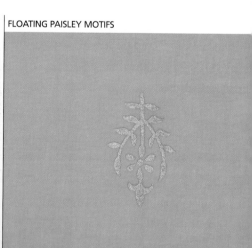

What to Shop for ▼

FURNITURE camelback sofas, cushioned swing chairs, and upholstered cotton dhurrie benches with turned wood legs | handcrafted sheesham or mango wood armchairs with loose cushions, dining tables, dining chairs, and buffets | British Colonial-style plantation tray tables, dining tables, plantation chairs, and four-poster beds | carved elephant coffee tables, trunks, tables, umbrella stands, and cabinets | hand-carved wood cabinets and wine racks | hand-painted, carved, and forged iron floor screens, trunks, and boxes

WINDOW TREATMENTS white crinkle voile, white on white applique or embroidered tab-top panels | shutters | cotton jacquard or velvet panels

SOFT FURNISHINGS bandhani tie-dyed, chappai block-printed, quilted, fabric appliqued, embroidered, or mirrorworked pillows, floor cushions, tablecloths, bed linens, and throws | cotton dhurrie and chindi rugs, phoolwari (field of flowers) flatwoven wool carpets | chenille rugs | coir or grass mats

TABLETOP FURNISHINGS indigo blue star-pattern plates, silver trays, and chargers | colored glass china, stemware, and glasses | iron candelabra

LIGHTING forged iron table and floor lamps, candelabra | colored glass or wire mesh lanterns | beaded votive cups, hooks for hanging mini lanterns

EMBROIDERED MIRRORWORK

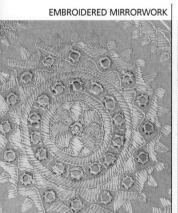

FEATHERS AND FRINGES

EMBROIDERY

COTTON WEAVES

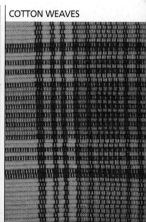

Abbey Style

KEYS TO THE STYLE

STRIP AWAY EXCESS. See the basics of daily life as everyday wonders. The goal of this style is open, uncluttered rooms. To furnish the "simple life," remove possessions that have no usefulness or meaning for you. Purge and give everything you don't need to people who do.

FIND COMFORT IN SIMPLICITY. Revel in the luxury of open, airy spaces. Decorate walls with light colors and vertical lines (tall, thin bands or broad, simple stripes in closely related colors emphasize height). Reflective surfaces and wide-open windows invite the sun to come in and shift shadows about the space.

CHOOSE PLAIN FURNITURE. Humble pieces, such as a long monastery-style table, a standard mattress and box springs, and straight-lined sofas or "church" chairs, are core pieces for the style. Accessories on the table, the bed, and around the seating pieces complete it.

THRILL THE MIND. While televisions and computers are necessary components of modern life, so are printed words that inspire and capture your imagination. Abbey style cultivates a thoughtful life of rooms filled with books, newspapers, magazines, and music. It also values handwritten letters or journals for recording personal histories.

ACCESSORIZE WITH SYMBOLS. Because the meditative life is central to this style, icons, books, and bibelots serve as this style's decorative jewelry. You'll find Gothic-shaped crosses, mirrors, frames, and new "cathedral salvage"—columns, windows, and architraves—in hobby, garden, and import stores.

A STANDARD SECTIONAL SOFA, CLAD IN A WASHABLE WHITE LINEN SLIPCOVER AND FURNISHED WITH WHITE CUSHIONS, INVITES READING, ARMCHAIR TRAVELS, AND QUIET RELAXATION. TRANSPARENT PANELS GENTLY DIVIDE THE LIVING AND DINING SPACES.

Living

Draw decorating inspiration from the halls and walls of ancient abbeys or cathedrals to bring home peace, tranquility, and time for reflection. A bit like "undecorating," abbey style cuts a living room to essentials, providing a place to sit, read, write, dream, or quietly relate to another.

Paint walls white or cover them with light paneling, wallcoverings, and high wainscots. In an open-plan space, hang transparent floor-to-ceiling curtain panels to divide living areas and create a mystical, dreamlike atmosphere. The goal for abbey style decorating is a home that transports you from the rat race, fast-pace working world.

For a life of contemplation and traveling in your mind, assemble bookcases and reading corners. Fill shelves with intriguing titles that beg to be read. Add books made by hand with hand-stitched pages and soft, porous papers that long for your handwritten notes and musings. Add seating pieces where you can spend hours comfortably cushioned and visually pleased with the room around you (washable white slipcovers bring old but comfortable upholstered pieces back to grace).

To light the space, use recessed lighting for its barely there presence. Place reading corners near large windows for the best light. In the evening substitute halogen task lamps for the most natural light. Candlelight is purely for effect, bringing your living spaces an ancient ambience and symbolizing the way things might have been at the abbey.

A READY-TO-ASSEMBLE "MADE-IN-ITALY" WRITING DESK CAME FROM AN IMPORT STORE. THE SEAT IS SOLD AS A TABLE.

Abbey style dining is usually a communal affair, although there are times when a meal eaten in solitude and serenity is welcome too.

Time is a luxury afforded the abbey style dining room, a chance to decorate the table with dishes and flowers, study it, and enjoy the arrangement as a still life while the table isn't in use. Make a long table the centerpiece of any room where you dine, whether it's a narrow coffee table or one long enough to seat 12. Situate tables parallel or perpendicular to walls for an orderly, semi-austere room arrangement.

A plain white tablecloth goes a long way toward expanding the elegance and grace of any table, no matter what its size or condition. For a rich look, cover the table with a layer of white felt before you lay out the cloth.

White dishes mark a table with perfection and purity, which is why most restaurants prefer them. White symbolizes cleanliness, giving those who eat from white plates a sense of pure and perfect food. Visually, too, the advantage of plain whiteware is clear—patterned dishes compete with and detract from the beauty of the food they serve, while white plates on silver chargers frame food like beautiful pictures.

For textural thrills add glasses with ribs or designs cut into their sides. Fill ironstone, porcelain, or china pitchers and bowls with greenery and place them where their heights won't interfere with conversation.

SEE GARDEN BENCHES AS PEWS AND ARRANGE THEM WITH ORDERED, CHURCHLIKE SYMMETRY.

TRANSFORM A WOODEN PICNIC TABLE WITH BENCH SEATING FOR ABBEY STYLE DINING: COVER THE TABLE WITH A LONG, WHITE CLOTH AND ADD A RUNNER OF CANDLES, PEWTER, AND FRAGILE STEMWARE. A GOTHIC MIRROR ON THE WALL RECALLS CATHEDRAL WINDOWS AND THE THRILL OF AWE-INSPIRING SPACES. ▼

Dining

COMMON THREADS, SUCH AS COTTON, LINEN, FELT, AND WOOL, GO INTO BEDMAKING. THIS HEADBOARD IS LITTLE MORE THAN MOLDINGS APPLIED TO DRYWALL TO GET THE LOOK OF CATHEDRAL-STYLE CHOIR STALL PANELING.

Sleeping

Slip away every night to a private sanctuary of pure white sheets. Whisper your wishes into the ears of angels.

PRACTICE MINIMALISM ON YOUR NIGHTSTAND BY TURNING A CHARGER INTO A "COLLECTION PLATE" ON TOP OF A GARDEN COLUMN. ▲

▼ BANISH THE CHILL WITH TEXTURAL, TRANSLUCENT FABRICS. ORGANDY AND EYELET BED CURTAINS FILTER THE LIGHT, CREATING A FEELING OF WARMTH WITHOUT WEIGHT.

A bed is the center of your bedroom and, more than likely, your favorite spot in the house. Place your bed in full view of the door so it is the focal point of the room. You'll need little more for furniture, simply some storage for clothing, bedside tables, reading lamps, curtains, and bedside rugs. A headboard and an end-of-the-bed bench are luxuries to symbolize and imitate furnishings found in real-life abbeys. Side curtains or triptych screens can close up spaces around the bed for more warmth, intimacy, or a sense of defined space.

Feather your nest with materials that promise rest and renewal. The basics—cotton cable-knit throws, ticking pillow and mattress protectors, chambray sheets, chenille bedspreads, down pillows or duvets, flannel or wool blankets, linen bed skirts, and lace trims—serve you well. Choose whites or pale neutrals in these materials for the most visually restful effect. Like a soft cloud on a breeze, a white surround of ceiling, walls, window coverings, and bedding takes you up and away to the world of dreams.

Details make a difference

Make Peace ▲

CREATE ORDER ON BOOKSHELVES WITH BIRDS OF PEACE. LOOK FOR HEAVY STONE BIRDS IN HOBBY AND CRAFTS STORES THAT CARRY DECORATIVE ACCESSORIES.

Break Bread ▲

FOR BUFFETS CHOOSE DECORATIVE SERVING PIECES MADE FROM IRON, BASKETS, GLASS, OR TERRA-COTTA. FILL A MEDIEVAL-STYLE BEE CATCHER *CENTER* WITH SWEET SYRUP TO LURE PICNIC PESTS AWAY.

Reflect

A MIRROR ENHANCES CANDLELIGHT ON AN OUTDOOR BUFFET. TO REFLECT THE SCENE, PLACE A MIRRORED BUFFET ACROSS FROM A TREE FILLED WITH STRANDS OF WHITE LIGHTS. STAND LONG TAPER CANDLES IN HOLDERS AT THE BOTTOM OF A GALVANIZED BUCKET PACKED WITH SHAVED ICE. ADD GLASSWARE FOR SPARKLE AND A BOUQUET OF WHITE FLOWERS, WHICH SHOW MORE BRIGHTLY IN CANDLELIGHT THAN BLOOMS OF ANOTHER COLOR.

Planning the Look

COLOR A broad selection of pale neutrals, whites, woody browns, and stony grays pull together this soft and subtle palette. A wealth of choices wait in paint stores, fabric stores, home centers, and discount markets. Quiet and serene, this color palette depends on pattern and texture for interest.

PATTERN Remember to be reserved when choosing patterns. It's a rare pattern that suits abbey style. Only the plainest patterns—embroidered crosses, handwriting, or gridded patterns of single motifs—give you the desired effect.

TEXTURE A feast of textures achieves the look. Get a feel for the style by collecting swatches of smooth white cottons, rustic ticking, soft chambrays, thirsty dish towels, fuzzy flannel, slubbed linen, transparent voile, and thick wool. Most of the warmth and comfort of this style comes with the fabrics you layer over plain surfaces. Create subtle contrasts of materials when setting tables, making beds, or displaying books. For example, if you choose smooth white china (rather than rustic pottery), set it against a rough burlap table runner with fringed ends. Arrange shelves with stacks of white, black, and gilt-edged book covers to create an enchanting environment. Add intrigue with carved surfaces of garden ornaments. Then tantalize with barely there sheers.

WHITE-ON-WHITE WEAVES

SISAL

EMBROIDERED CROSSES

126

STONE AGGREGATE

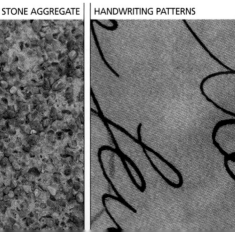

HANDWRITING PATTERNS

What to **Shop** for

▼

FURNITURE straight-lined sofa and chairs slipcovered with washable white linen, cotton, or canvas | small writing desk, bookcases | wood benches with and without backs, folding "church" chairs with straight lines | picnic tables and benches or expandable rectangular tables | church pews or parson's chairs with white upholstery | white metal end tables, serving carts

WINDOW TREATMENTS pleated paper shades | roller shades | standard white sheers | voile or Indian cotton tab-top curtains on white poles | white cafe curtains, rice paper shades | white wood blinds

SOFT FURNISHINGS white cotton duvets, sheets, pillowcases, tablecloths, napkins, and toss pillows | terry cloth bath towels and bath mats | rectangular floor cushions with white covers | white cotton dish towels, brown burlap table runners or mats | sisal, jute, or cotton rugs

TABLETOP FURNISHINGS plain white china, earthenware, or stoneware | stainless-steel flatware, pots, pans, and silver chargers | faceted glasses and stemware | candle mats, green plants | pewter serving pieces

LIGHTING church candles, votive lights | crystal chandeliers | recessed lighting/wall washers | halogen lamps | iron candlestands, bobeches

TRANSPARENT WEAVES | MONK'S CLOTH | CARVED "STONE" | HOPSACKING

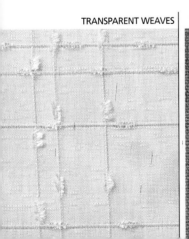

Swedish Lite

KEYS TO THE STYLE

■**NEUTRALIZE WALLS AND FLOORS.**
Create light and airy envelopes of space that invite sunshine in. Ivory white paint and pale woods, such as birch, ash, and beech, are always right in any room, although you could mix it up a little with an occasional pale blue, green, or yellow painted wall. Keep window coverings wispy, too, so optimum light enters the house.

■**INCORPORATE WHITE BONES.**
Structure each room with furniture basics that continue the neutral tones of the walls, windows, ceilings, and floors. For living, you need a sofa and chairs with washable ivory-white canvas covers and white or wood tables and freestanding storage. For dining, buy wood and/or white tables, chairs, and freestanding storage. For sleeping, add beds and pull together white, wood, and glass-fronted freestanding storage units, bedside tables, and lounging chairs.

■**ADD A LAYER OF COLOR.** Once the basics of room design are in place, let the decorating begin! Kick up the visual interest with fabrics laid over plain surfaces. Lay rugs over floors to define a space and roll a runner down a hallway. Soften sofas with cushions, then enrich tables with tablecloths. Introduce pattern with dishcloths, napkins, window treatments, and bedding.

■**ACCENT WITH RED.** In neutralized spaces layered with medium-tone colors, a shot of red will bring things to life. Cherry red, a favorite of Scandinavians, is used for the sheer joy of the power it brings to a room. Red is the symbol for love, energy, hearts, and hospitality.

■**ADD ART.** Use framed pictures, glassware, or white porcelain massed for impact on open shelves. Another idea: Hang free-form modern plastic sculptures midair.

GRAY-TONED PASTELS AND IVORY BLEND TOGETHER IN A WHISPER-QUIET SPACE FOR GATHERING. THE CENTRAL FOCUS IS
A COFFEE TABLE EQUIPPED WITH A HANDY SHELF. A RED AND CREAM WOVEN RUG WARMS THE WHITE-PAINTED FLOOR
THAT SUBTLY LIFTS THE MOOD OF THE SPACE. ▼

Living

Swedish Lite is a decorating diet with a low-fat plan that gets your rooms looking lean, sleek, and sophisticated yet warm and inviting. It's a look that begins with white, a natural for washing rooms with freshness and drawing in as much natural light as possible through windows.

If your home lacks natural light and you like fresh and friendly gatherings and open-plan living, this may be the look for you. Mostly modern, this historic style also carries a few traditional marks: new furniture pieces inspired by 18th century Gustavian furnishings, delicate carved wood accents, and fabrics with pretty floral prints or embroidered motifs.

For the contemporary side of Swedish living, treat walls and floors with paint or hardwood. New light-colored wood laminate flooring (no carpet for this look) is an excellent product with practical, durable, and washable pluses. For an even lighter, airier feel, paint floorboards with hard-wearing white deck paint. Buy basic, straight-lined upholstery seating pieces with washable white canvas slipcovers, white or light wood tables, white floor-to-ceiling curtain panels, and contemporary stainless-steel halogen lamps.

For traditional touches that add familiarity and warmth, add splashes of color with cushions covered in narrow stripes and organized floral prints, an area rug, handblown curvy glassware, and humorous accents such as polka dots or plastic spirals.

SHELVES STACKED FLOOR TO CEILING CREATE VERTICAL STORAGE. VIBRANT COLORS SPARKLE IN A WHITE SPACE.

The heart of this home is a long dining table that extends to seat many. Choose a light-colored wood table that has leaves to snap in place.

Cut decorating costs by shopping the aisles of supermarket-style decorating stores for modern Scandinavian pieces you can assemble yourself. Stock up on white laminate or wood shelves for open storage, Swedish towel racks, a multitude of paintable wooden dining chairs with straight lines, and a bench or two.

Paint walls in barely there pastels that have slightly grayed-down tones ("simple sophistication" is often created with complexities and subtle nuances). Historically Swedes matched their pastel palettes to the slightly grayed hues of cool, northerly skies and wide open seas.

Accent with red. Paint a few unfinished furniture pieces red and purchase useful dining accessories that bring energy to tabletops and open shelves you've hung on the walls. Be sure to lace the displays with lots of white to keep the look light and bright.

Less is best for windows. Uncovered panes bring in the most light and a modern look. However a fabric shade, plain white sheer panels, or white wood blinds soften edges and are perfect solutions for maximum light control and a bit of privacy.

LINE UP TWO WALL-HUNG SHELVES, A TOWEL RACK, AND A PAIR OF CHAIRS TO SUGGEST A TRADITIONAL CUPBOARD.

Dining ▲

ENHANCED WITH RED ACCENTS, THIS DINING ROOM HAS A WARM AND
FRIENDLY ATTITUDE. AT THE SAME TIME, IT HAS A CLUTTER-FREE AUSTERITY
THAT'S TYPICALLY SCANDINAVIAN.

THREE LAYERS OF FABRIC AT THE WINDOW HELP CREATE THIS COZY SLEEPING ROOM. LAYER ONE IS A WHITE SHEER PANEL WHILE LAYERS TWO AND THREE ARE REALLY A PAIR OF CAFE CURTAINS STACKED ONE OVER THE OTHER ON STANDARD TENSION RODS.

Sleeping

The down duvet is king of bed fittings in northern climates. You can buy summer-weight versions for less warmth and beat allergies with cotton or wool alternatives.

When you're using duvets, a patterned duvet cover rules the room's decor. Begin by purchasing a duvet cover to play a focal-point role in the scheme. It should inspire your decorating energies and guide your choices for the remaining parts of the room. Some covers come with coordinating linens that simplify the task of choosing fabrics.

Draw ideas and colors for the room from the prints or patterns of the bed linens. Does a pattern inspire light humor in the room? A tailored look? Romantic choices? In the room *right* a red and white duvet cover inspired a red and white scheme. Like the base color of the duvet, white became the base color for the room. Red, like the hearts, became the accent color for sheets, TV cushions, and a row of pots. A woven runner with dense stripes counters the curved lines and shapes to complete the love nest.

The bedroom *opposite* took decorating lessons from coordinating linens. A related fabric (not part of the linen collection) found at a fabric store softens a bedside table. The blue-painted walls come from the base color of the linens. Yellow curtains, a color not drawn from the fabric prints, softly contrasts and accents the red, blue, and white palette.

HEARTS, SO OFTEN SWEET, APPEAR HERE IN GLIB, CARTOONY ROWS ON A DUVET COVER.

Details make a difference

A Touch of Red

USE RED AS A DETAIL COLOR ON LAMPSHADES, COZY QUILTS, A TABLECLOTH, BENCH, OR PILLOW COVERS. TEAMED WITH WHITE OR PALE COLORS, THE BRILLIANCE OF RED IS HEIGHTENED, TURNING UP THE HEAT AND ENERGY LEVEL IN THE ROOM.

Bath Spa

ADAPT THE SCANDINAVIAN SAUNA LOOK WITH WOOD-PANELED WALLS AND A TUBSIDE TABLE THAT'S REALLY A GUSTAVIAN-STYLE CHAIR. INSTEAD OF TAKING THE SCANDI-STYLE PLUNGE INTO ICY WATERS, BABY YOURSELF WITH TEXTURED TOWELS, CANDLELIT BATHS, AND LOTS OF FRESH-SCENTED SOAP.

Tabletop Lights

FOR MAGICAL EVENINGS OR EARLY
MORNING GATHERINGS AROUND A TABLE,
ARRANGE A ROW OF CERAMIC VOTIVE
CANDLEHOLDERS IN A CURVE. SOMETIMES
YOU CAN FIND A SERIES OF HOLDERS
HELD TOGETHER WITH FLEXIBLE BANDS
WHICH MAKES LINING UP CANDLES QUICK
AND EASY TO DO.

Cross-Stitch Motifs

INCLUDE TRADITIONAL HANDMADE
TOUCHES, LIKE THIS TINY HORSE,
CROSS-STITCHED AT THE TOP OF A RED
PILLOW COVER. WORK IT YOURSELF OR
BUY IT READY-MADE.

Planning the Look

COLOR When gathering paint choices, use the color strip *above* as a guide. Include an ivory white for basic use on walls and woodwork throughout the house. At the paint rack, you'll see that blues and greens come in varying grades of brilliance and clarity. Select slightly grayed-down pastels for authentic Swedish coloring. Pale yellow is good for rooms where people gather. Blues and greens emphasize rest in bedrooms. White is right anywhere.

PATTERN The walls of Swedish rooms are plain or textured with wood paneling and/or floorboards. Patterns work their ways into room schemes on fabrics (upholstery, Roman shades, dish towels, bed linens, pillows, throws, and rugs) in crisp checks, striped patterns of varying widths, organized flower prints, gridded geometrics, or traditional, old-world two-color toiles, and paisleys.

TEXTURE Swedish Lite textures are fairly mute in a room where patterns layer color over walls and floors. The main texture is smooth, sleek, and shiny with surfaces that are easily cleaned and free from clutter. Occasionally you'll find ribs on smooth, creamy porcelain dishes, matte finishes on stainless-steel flatware, and rustic weaves on rugs and table runners. Look for subtle textures: frosted glass, transparent blown glass, or a basket weave.

FLORAL-PRINT FABRICS | GRIDDED PATTERNS | HEAVILY WOVEN COTTONS AND WOOLS

138

What to Shop for

FURNITURE straight-lined sofas and chairs upholstered in washable canvas or slipcovers | finished or unfinished wood dining chairs and benches | paintable wicker side chairs | light wood, glass, metal, or white-painted tables for dining, sofa, and chairside | light wood or white laminate wall-hung shelving; freestanding storage—wardrobes, armoires, bookcases, and entertainment centers | straight-lined wood or metal headboards

WINDOW TREATMENTS streamlined Roman shades | white floor-to-ceiling curtain tab-top or grommeted panels of voile, muslin, or cotton | white, wood, or metal blinds | 3-tiered cafe curtains | swagged pelmets

SOFT FURNISHINGS bright-colored duvets, sheets, pillowcases, and table linens | woven table runners, floor runners, and area rugs | crisp two-tone checks, plaids, and floral prints on cushions, kitchen linens, and chair slips

TABLETOP FURNISHINGS plain cream-colored porcelain dishes with ribbed surfaces | enamelware, wood, or metal serving pieces, baskets, and trays | standard clear glasses and stemware | streamlined stainless-steel flatware

LIGHTING cable lighting | track lights | stainless-steel based floor, table, and desktop halogen fixtures | pendants with glass or plastic shades

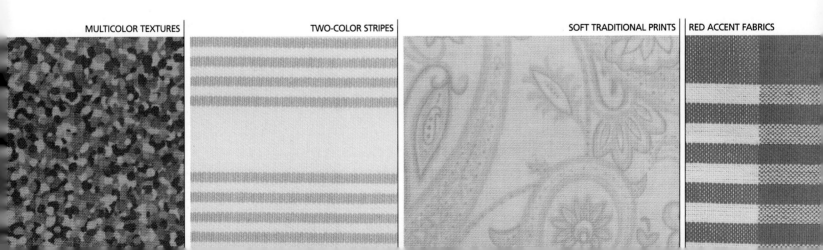

MULTICOLOR TEXTURES | TWO-COLOR STRIPES | SOFT TRADITIONAL PRINTS | RED ACCENT FABRICS

Loft Style

KEYS TO THE STYLE

■**RECOVER LOST SPACE.** Loft style rescues wood, marble, or travertine floors and walls of industrial spaces to make them livable for domestic life. For the modern gallery look of this chapter (you can adapt loft style to a suburban home), paint walls white. Then add a bright accent wall or a partition wall consisting of textured glass, metal, or plastic panels. Seal newly sanded floors with a light, clear stain. Leave windows bare or custom-fit them with roller blinds and pleated shades for daylight control.

■**DEFINE ZONES FOR LIVING.** Use area rugs to create "rooms." Divide open-plan spaces with furniture to form "walls" around living, sleeping, and dining functions. For flexibility choose lightweight pieces that are easy to rearrange.

■**GO MOD.** Multiples, such as modular storage pieces, form the architecture of loft "rooms." Some divide and conquer spaces that feel too large, wrapping around seating for comfort.

■**BE GRAPHIC.** Large spaces allow room for exaggerated aesthetics. Hang larger-than-life graphics that showcase brilliant colors or collect dozens of black and white posters to line and overlap each other along a wall. Exaggerate colors and textures too. Find lavish furnishings of silk, faux fur, cotton, linen, velvet, and suede. Hang fabric canvases silk-screened in bright, florid prints. Look for table linens worth more splash than cash.

■**SEE THE LIGHT.** When daylight retreats in the evening, replace it with manufactured lighting that has enough power to fill large spaces. Architecturally impressive fixtures and lights that double as shapely artworks fit a lofty style. For reading and task areas, be sure to add strong, directed high-tech lights. For soft mood lighting, distribute uplights along the floor behind plants or under tables.

THREE METAL READY-TO-ASSEMBLE SHELVING UNITS CREATE A "WALL" THAT DIVIDES THE LIVING AND DINING SPACES IN AN OPEN LOFT. ON THIS SIDE—THE LIVING SIDE—THE DIVIDER ACTS AS A BOOKCASE. TURN THE PAGE TO SEE HOW THE DIVIDER WORKS ON THE DINING SIDE.

Living

Loft living means sitting in the luxurious lap of high, wide-open spaces. Whether a loft space is recovered from a warehouse or an abandoned factory, it's likely to be made from outstanding materials. Creating a home from such rich industrial rubble is a modern delight.

With loft walls, ceiling, and floors exposed, you can treat their surfaces in a contemporary or traditional way. Smooth white walls and a bright accent wall or two promote a modern look while dark-toned brick walls, woods, crown moldings, and wainscots form a deep, warm cocoon of classicism.

In either case be flexible. Put loft space to use with lightweight furniture pieces that are easy to rearrange. Define living spaces with large area rugs and furniture groupings that you can change at will.

For storage, go urban with ready-to-assemble modular cubes and shelving units you can stack and arrange in a number of ways. Available in the aisles of mass-market stores, these storage cubes come with open shelves, doors, or drawers. For a sofa wrap, *right,* stack the storage pieces up to about the same height as the back of the sofa. Two rows of four boxes each stack behind the sofa. Each side unit is made from a 29-inch-long rectangular base unit topped by two side-by-side 14½-inch cubes. In the living room *opposite* cubes create a four-square coffee table, a between-two-sofas table, and end tables. Everything can shift if space is needed elsewhere.

MODULAR CUBES HIDE CLUTTER IN PLAIN SIGHT WHILE PROVIDING FLAT SURFACES FOR SOCIABLE LIVING. ▲

Dream up loft dining with casual and formal attitudes—you'll have room for both. Open spaces with flexible furniture make way for any number of configurations, guests, and notable occasions.

In today's broadband world, a dining room is a welcome oasis from meals on the run and regular restaurant stops. It's where you can recharge, refuel, and reconnect with family and friends before taking up the quick pace again.

Create several dining spots around your loft— a sort of menu of choices that fits different moods and schedules. For example, a stainless-steel or wood island or bar-height counter that divides the kitchen and living areas is a natural meeting and eating place any time of the day. A wealth of bar sets, stools, and bar-height chairs are available in the aisles of import, discount, and mass-market stores.

Big, square coffee tables (made from modular storage units) coupled with comfortable upholstery invite cushy dining in the living room with friends or alone in front of the big screen. If your desk is the hub of your living space, clear the work surface occasionally to serve as a walk-by buffet or wet bar.

Expand dining space for large parties with multiples of long, square, or round utility tables set in a loose arrangement or tight formation around the loft. Cover all tables with white restaurant-style tablecloths. With the sky's-the-limit space of a loft, you can host any number of grandiose occasions.

▲ STEEL AND GLASS FURNISHINGS, CONSTRUCTED IN SIMPLE GEOMETRY, FIT THE INDUSTRIAL FEEL OF A MODERN LOFT.

Dining

IMPORT-STORE POSTERS FRAMED IN BLACK METAL SERENDIPITOUSLY FIT THE STRUCTURE OF THESE METAL SHELVING UNITS. THE ART POSTER ON THE LIVING ROOM SIDE CREATES A BACK WALL FOR A CHINA CUPBOARD ON THIS SIDE. THE TWO POSTERS SHOWN HERE BACK THE BOOKCASES ON THE LIVING ROOM SIDE.

READY-TO-ASSEMBLE SHOE-STACKER UNITS FROM BED AND BATH STORES HANG UPSIDE DOWN ON A
BRIGHT PARTITION WALL. WHITE BOARDS FASTENED OVER THEIR BOTTOMS FORM A BED SURROUND.

Sleeping

Lie back in the light-filled luxury of wide-open spaces, contemporary quilts, and outdoor reflections pictured in large-size pier mirrors.

▼ WHITE-PAINTED WALLS ARE "PANELED" IN OVERSIZE RECTANGLES OF STRONG COLOR PAINTED OVER THE WHITE BACKGROUND. EIGHT-INCH GAPS OF WHITE BETWEEN THE PAINTED RECTANGLES EXTEND THE LOOK OF CROWN MOLDING DOWN THE WALL TO THE WIDE WHITE BASE AND FLOOR BELOW.

Some loft beds float like islands in an open sea of space. Others anchor themselves securely behind a divider wall to create a more private haven. The bed, often a low-lying mattress and box spring on a metal frame, speaks in Asian or minimalist tones. A slim, four-poster bed kit you assemble yourself is another option that defines the bed structurally and gives sleepers a sense of place or sanctuary, creating a small room within a big one. For an impressive headboard with plenty of handy storage, stack two or three rows of modular cubes behind the head of a bed. A daybed is a good sleeping solution for guests. A sofa by day and bed by night, the slipcovered daybed *left* possesses lofty luxury 24 hours a day.

Loft style requires barely visible storage, especially in the bedroom. Create wall-to-wall closets with multiples of freestanding wardrobes or modular closet units you assemble yourself. Another idea: Establish a headboard wall for the bed in an open space, leaving room behind it for a large walk-through closet (you can enter from either side of the bed). Then move in modular units, hanging racks, or ready-to-assemble closet storage. If desired create back-to-back closets in the space behind the headboard wall, one for each bed partner.

Few other bedroom furnishings are needed for this clutter-free style. Just add bedside tables, a chaise or chair, and an area rug to soften the floor. Install lighting by fastening reading lamps to the wall above the bed.

Details make a difference

Coffee Table, Nested ▲

BUY TWO SETS OF NESTING TABLES WITH THREE
TABLES IN EACH SET. PLACE THE TWO TALLEST TABLES
NEAR THE CENTER OF THE COFFEE TABLE SPACE. THEN
ADD THE REMAINING TABLES AT THEIR SIDES AND
ENDS IN A PLEASING ARRANGEMENT THAT LEAVES
STORAGE SLOTS ON THE FLOOR FOR BOOKS.

Blue Bottles, Massed ▲

WASH LABELS FROM COBALT BLUE WINE AND WATER BOTTLES. GROUP
THEM TOGETHER ON A SIDEBOARD OR WALL-HUNG SHELF FOR A
DISPLAY WITH PLENTY OF IMPACT.

Coffee Table, Cubed ▲

ASSEMBLE TWO STORAGE CUBES—ONE WITH SHELVES, THE OTHER
WITH A DOOR. ADD FEET (THESE READY-TO-ASSEMBLE UNITS COME
WITH OPTIONAL METAL FEET, WHICH ADD ABOUT 4 INCHES IN
HEIGHT). PAIR THEM UP IN FRONT OF A SOFA.

Bookcase, Stacked ▲

TWO OPEN CUBES, A CUBE WITH DRAWERS,
ANOTHER WITH A DOOR, AND A FIFTH WITH A
SHELF ADD UP TO A BOOKCASE SERVING A
READING CORNER.

Planning the Look

COLOR Be bold. Think bright, clear, and saturated when planning colors for a loft scheme. First choose a basic white for walls (compare whites at the paint store rack and select one that is neither too yellow, too pink, nor too blue). Then choose a primary color as a main theme to repeat throughout the loft. Choose two more hues from the color guide *above* to supplement the main color. Add black to provide contrast to the white walls and to delineate colors.

PATTERN When choosing fabrics, select more plain than patterned. When choosing a pattern, go graphic with giant flowers on a bedspread, a stunning striped rug, or a bold geometric piece of framed art to play the leading role as an aesthetic focal point. For finer patterning go with small geometric checks and stripes or black and white photography.

TEXTURE With a single, strong pattern on pillow covers or framed art in the lead, large-scale textures balance the modern mix by bringing softness, interest, and variety to it. Go seductive with a flokati rug. Put suede, leather, or velvet fabrics on floor cushions, slipcovers, or curtains. Bring in a corrugated metal wall as a backdrop, pinstripe a tailored daybed cover, and set out fuzzy succulent plants in galvanized metal buckets.

MARBLE, TRAVERTINE | MODERN ART | HEAVY WOVEN COTTONS

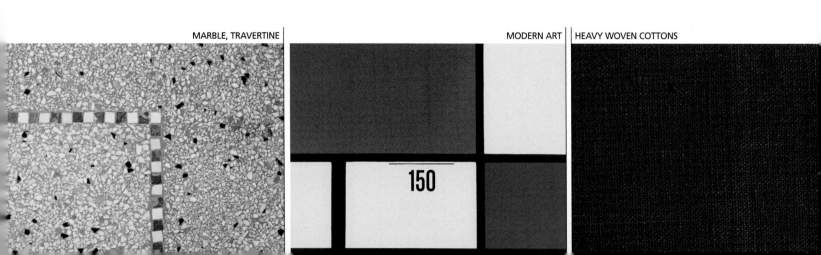

150

What to **Shop** for

FURNITURE straight-lined sofa and chairs upholstered in washable white canvas; bright slipcovers | iron/cane chairs | stainless-steel glass-topped tables, stainless-steel stools with vinyl upholstery | vinyl, metal, stainless-steel, or plywood tables | metal shelving | wood-finish or white laminate modular storage cubes for bookcases or coffee, sofa, end, and bedside tables

WINDOW TREATMENTS grommeted floor-to-ceiling cotton or sheer panels | custom roller shades | glass panes etched or frosted with geometric shapes | textured plastic panels hung over panes | stainless-steel or wood blinds

SOFT FURNISHINGS a mix of white and graphically-printed cotton or silk quilts, duvets, duvet covers, sheets, and pillowcases | leather shag rugs, area rugs with large graphic designs, rugs woven with bold bands of color | white canvas or boldly designed coverings on toss pillows | fake fur throws

TABLETOP FURNISHINGS plain white china, covered tureens, pitchers, and linens | stainless-steel flatware, pots, pans, and chargers | frosted glasses and stemware | serving platters with graphics printed on their surfaces

LIGHTING cable or track lighting | architectural table and floor lamps | contemporary metal floor lamps | stainless steel pendant lamps

GEOMETRICS RE-HABBED WOOD BOLD ABSTRACT PATTERNS CAMERA GRAPHICS

Tuscan Sun

KEYS TO THE STYLE

■ **GROUND YOUR VILLA.** Tuscan builders make practical use of indigenous materials from the surrounding landscape with walls and floors made from wood, brick, stucco, and stone. Rough-plastered walls are glazed with color washes and some wood floors are whitewashed to reflect the light. Other floors are tiled with sunbaked, terra-cotta tiles. Plan to incorporate as many of these rustic elements as possible.

■ **HARMONIZE WITH NATURE.** Tuscan style is all about finding cool shelter from the sun. Rooms that need warmth and light welcome the sun through Palladian-style windows reminiscent of Roman architecture. Open-air summer rooms usually face north for coolness. Wood shutters controlling the flow of light into rooms are an essential component of this style. For a practical (and elegant) window treatment, hang floor-to-ceiling drapery panels of linen fabric over large windows.

■ **CHOOSE RUSTIC FURNITURE.** Farmhouse-style furniture with a handcrafted look—a long table is the most essential—consists of wooden chests and credenzas for storage, tables, chairs, benches, and stools. Long armrests, retained from Renaissance days, are typical on chairs and settees. Seats of peasant-style chairs are woven, and their straight backs are usually composed of two vertical stiles connected by two or three horizontal slats. Wicker and wrought iron (a traditional Tuscan craft) are two more furniture choices.

■ **CHOOSE NATURAL FIBERS.** Look for fabrics in simple, loose weaves, handmade lace, white on white embroidery, and a few plainly crocheted pieces. Count on majolica or glazed ceramics to provide pictorial focal points for rooms.

■ **ACCESSORIZE.** Use family pictures, candlesticks, green plants, pottery, green-glass bottles, and ceramic tiles.

THE CURVES OF WROUGHT-IRON AND WICKER FURNITURE PIECES
ECHO THE GRACEFUL ARC OF A FOCAL-POINT, MEDITERRANEAN-
STYLE WINDOW. TERRA-COTTA TILES ON THE FLOOR SUGGEST A
COOL, RELAXED ENVIRONMENT FOR A LEISURELY GATHERING.

Living

154

A toast to this convivial and gracious way of life—for a Tuscan Sun home is a symbol for offering hospitality, gathering friends, and creating vibrant conversations. Plan a table for food service in every living space because sharing food lies at the core of this relaxed and generous lifestyle.

Large, curved windows, stuccoed walls, iron gates, and brick fireplaces quickly establish a Mediterranean vibe. If this is the architectural style of your home—many American homes built in the 1970s bear the stamp—go with the flow. Giving your rooms the glow of agrarian Tuscany indulges the senses and warms the heart. Because this lifestyle is currently alive and well, you'll find plenty of decorating inspiration and motivation. If your home lacks Mediterranean-style architecture, you can find ways to build it in by rough-plastering or colorwashing walls, by tiling floors, backsplashes, and countertops, or by installing new windows.

For living spaces bring on the seating—you'll need lots of it. Authentic Tuscan living spaces feature exposed wood, wrought-iron, and wicker frames with loose-cushion upholstery. Choose cushions with plain covers in a variety of Italian colors (see pages 162–163). Hang simple floor-to-ceiling linen drapes or hinge shutters on windows.

Accessorize with green plants and classically shaped earthenware pots. Look for tall and short urn shapes that bring back the feel of classical Rome. Be sentimental and feature family pictures on open shelves, mantels, and tabletops. Include favorite candlesticks and green-glass wine bottles in displays. Light the candles for social gatherings and special occasions that celebrate the family.

For lighting, choose lamps with terra-cotta or clay bases that resemble the classical urn-shaped pots you select for green plants. Top the bases with white shades.

EXPOSED-FRAME WICKER SOFAS AND A CHUNKY WOOD COFFEE TABLE SETTLE IN FRONT OF A BRICK FIREPLACE. ▲

Because cooking and enjoying food are cornerstones of Tuscan Sun style, kitchens are large with space for a good-size table. Dining rooms are best when their spirits and decor match the casual attitude and impromptu nature of family and neighborhood gatherings.

Invest in a table for every room in the house—each one will enjoy heavy use. You'll love a long harvest table for dinner in an open-plan space (think of Tuscan field workers gathering for the noon meal). Seat everyone on long wood benches or a collection of farmhouse chairs with woven rush bottoms. In kitchens round or square tables work well for spontaneous gatherings; for other sit-back-and-enjoy spaces, buy large wooden coffee tables or wrought-iron tables with glass or ceramic-tiled tops.

Tuscan Sun style loves open storage that shows off the utilitarian elements of cooking and dining. Decorate walls with plain colors as a wise backdrop for displaying dishes and cookware. Buy baker's racks, freestanding cupboards, shelving units, and hanging racks for pots and pans. Hang spice racks under shelves and stash unattractive (but useful) bits and pieces in woven baskets on open shelves. Buy earthenware dishes glazed in Tuscan colors (see pages 162–163) and decorated with fruit and vine patterns to resemble majolica. Display the largest pieces in the most prominant places for decorative focal points.

For table coverings look for plain linen pieces, geometric plaids, or fabrics woven in two-color miniature checks.

▲ A WROUGHT-IRON BAKER'S RACK PROVIDES STORAGE SPACE IN EITHER THE KITCHEN OR THE DINING ROOM.

A MIX OF ONE-OF-A-KIND CHAIRS IN A VARIETY OF FARMHOUSE SHAPES COMES TOGETHER AROUND A LIGHTLY-OILED PINE KITCHEN TABLE WHERE FOOD PREPARATION AS WELL AS OFF-THE-CUFF GATHERINGS HAPPEN.

Dining

157

MELLOW YELLOW WALLS AND TWO SETS OF BIFOLD SHUTTERED DOORS SET THE BACKDROP FOR A RUSTIC, COUNTRIFIED
BED FRAME AND SIMPLE WHITE BEDDING. A MATELASSE BEDCOVER IS A TYPICAL CHOICE FOR COOL SLEEPING.
MATCHSTICK BLINDS, FRAMED IN WHITE PINE, LAYER TEXTURE OVER WHITE PAPER SHADES.

Sleeping

Whisper the word "spare" to yourself
while gathering the elements of your
Tuscan Sun bedroom.

▼ CONTEMPORARY MACHINED LACE ON BED LINENS FROM
DISCOUNT STORE AISLES IMITATE AUTHENTIC OLD-WORLD
HANDMADE LACES REMARKABLY WELL.

Little time is spent in the bedroom when you're occupied with Tuscan-style gatherings and cooking great food. The bedroom stands for a cool respite from the sun with midday siestas. It's an uncomplicated space that rests eyes and revives spirits overnight. Window coverings—shutters rather than curtains—cut back the sunlight, provide privacy, and add more variety to the textural accents of rough-plaster walls and white-painted floorboards.

Bedding is airy, light, and fresh. A neutral color scheme assures tranquility while sweet laces and down-to-earth materials keep it countrified rather than slick, smooth, or sophisticated. Although authentic Tuscan bedding is handmade, you can substitute inexpensive machined goods from discount stores. Look for hotel sheet sets for basics. Then find a bedskirt with ribbon lace and a decorator table set made with whitework embroidery, cutwork, and scalloped edges. Splurge on delicate lace-trimmed pillow shams and standard pillowcases with inset bands of ribbon lace. You can mix and match a variety of laces and textures successfully when you choose all-white pieces.

Top off the bed with a lightweight panel of taupe and white matelassé for a slight contrast of color. You'll recognize matelassé in shopping aisles by its tight weave and organized repeated motifs.

159

Details make a difference

Boot Chair ▲

STATION A RUSTIC FARMHOUSE CHAIR NEAR A DOOR
FOR CONVENIENT SEATING WHILE PULLING OFF OR
PUTTING ON YOUR BOOTS. NOTE THE WICKER
SEAT AND CHUNKY FRAME THAT TYPIFIES TUSCAN
SUN STYLE.

Bottle Vases ▲

RECYCLE EMPTIED GREEN-GLASS OLIVE OIL BOTTLES WITH ATTRACTIVE
LABELS (FIND THEM IN IMPORT-MARKET STORES) TO USE AS
IMPROMPTU TUSCAN SUN STYLE VASES. THE BOTTLES, WHEN FILLED
WITH FLOWERS, ALSO MAKE ATTRACTIVE HOST OR HOSTESS GIFTS TO
BRING TO A DINNER PARTY.

Sun Spot ▲

TUSCAN SUN STYLE SPILLS THROUGH THE
DOORS OF THE HOUSE TO SHADY TERRACES.
EXTEND YOUR LIVING QUARTERS OUTWARD
ON ANY AVAILABLE PATIO, DECK, TERRACE, OR
SMOOTH CONCRETE SURFACE YOU CAN.
DECORATE WITH REAL OR FAUX TILE,
WROUGHT-IRON PLANTERS, AND GARDEN
CHAIRS. WHEN PAINTING ON CONCRETE, BE
SURE TO CLEAN THE SURFACE THOROUGHLY
BEFORE APPLYING A GRID OF MASKING TAPE
THAT OUTLINES THE DESIGN. PAINT THE DESIGN
IN DECK PAINT AND REMOVE THE TAPE.

Smooth Treads ▲

USING A STAPLE GUN, FASTEN INEXPENSIVE TOSS RUGS IN SMALL-SCALE,
REPEATED-MOTIF WEAVES AROUND OPEN STAIRSTEPS OR OVER THE
STEPS OF A CLOSED STAIRCASE. OVERLAP ENDS NEATLY ON THE
UNDERSIDES OR EDGES.

Planning the Look

▼

COLOR Gather sun-drenched paint and wood-stain samples using the color strip *above* as a guide. Plan to feature no more than three colors in any room—the quickest way to capture the rustic decorative style of the Mediterranean countryside. For a fun dimension of Tuscan style, learn about artists' colors in art and crafts supply stores. Some colors from this earthy palette are named for Italian towns and cities; many are found in Italian frescos.

PATTERN Few decorative patterns are desirable for this style. Use a botanical or repeated pattern on key upholstery cushions as a focus fabric in a room. For supplementary cushions and curtains, choose plain-colored fabrics with loose, textural weaves. Lemon-and-vine or olive-and-leaf motifs are typical patterns for china. Patterned wallcoverings aren't authentic to this style but could be used if they imitate the look of colorwashing, rough whitewash, stone, wrought iron, or brick. When buying wrought-iron furniture, select those with scroll patterns.

TEXTURE Stress texture, rather than pictorial pattern, to get the rural look of Tuscany. Use rough-weave fabrics, handmade lace, crocheted mats, rugs, and runners. Stucco, rough plaster, ceramic, brick, and stone surfaces are desirable textures on walls and floors.

WOVEN RUSH | NATURAL COTTON CROCHET | ORGANIZED REPEATS

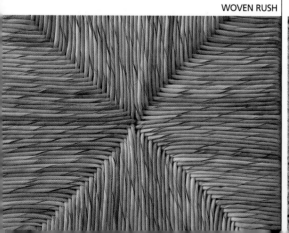

What to Shop for

FURNITURE chunky farmhouse-style pine chairs with rush seats | wicker chairs and settees with loose-cushion upholstery | rectangular or long, wooden harvest tables, wood chairs, garden benches with exposed frames | wrought-iron baker's racks, garden settees with cushions, mosaic-topped patio table and chair sets | wood/rush stools | chunky wood coffee, side, and bedside tables | wood or wrought-iron bed frames

WINDOW TREATMENTS shutters | natural linen draperies | white cotton sheers | embroidered cotton curtain panels | wood miniblinds

SOFT FURNISHINGS seat cushions and toss pillows of natural fibers in naive, loose patterns for upholstery | crochet table mats | linen, matelessé, handmade lace, or embroidered white cotton linens and curtains | sea grass or rush area rugs, sisal carpet, woven cotton runners and dhurrie rugs

TABLETOP FURNISHINGS glazed earthenware, stoneware, terra-cotta | woven baskets lined with linens | copper pots and pans | green glassware | wood cutting boards and serving trays, fringed tablecloths and napkins

LIGHTING lamps with classic pottery bases | ginger jar lamps with white shades | candlesticks, candles in hurricane jars | wrought-iron chandeliers

CERAMIC TILE | RIBBON LACE | SIMPLE PLAIDS | WOVEN CHECKS

New Traditional

KEYS TO THE STYLE

MODERNIZE BACKDROPS. Replace complicated antique glazes, expensive gold glitz, and heavy, upholstered walls with freshly painted walls in soul-soothing colors and simplified decorating that doesn't require designer services. You can create a classic, timeless style with your own capable hands and the guideposts outlined in this chapter.

SEEK KNOWLEDGE. Traditional furniture styles carry their lines from generation to generation. Bone up on the history of furniture shapes developed between the Georgian period (1700s) and the Arts and Crafts Movement (late 1800s to early 1900s) in America. Whether you favor Queen Anne, Gustavian, or American Colonial style, equip your mind and eye for informed shopping.

FAST FORWARD. Search store aisles and practice window-shopping and you'll find the new classics that will get you the streamlined look of your favorite traditional style.

FIND COMMON GROUND. A neutral color palette, the first source of continuity between traditional and modern styles, is the perfect starting point. From there develop a profile (palette) of materials possessing integrity—polished wood, metal, and glass, variegated wicker, wrought iron, mirror, and fabrics of refinement. Look for common patterns, drawn from geometrics and traditional leaf or toile patterns, that are enlarged to look more modern.

DISCRIMINATE. Purchase furnishings with a curator's eye, cutting away choices that confuse or clutter. Choose furniture pieces of distinctive size to avoid the dollhouse look and attain a simplified, modern feel. Create a single focal point in each room, directing all remaining pieces to and around it. Trust your instincts to tell you when enough is enough or if something more is needed to complete the room.

Living

WALLS BANDED WITH GRADUATING NEUTRAL TONES SUPPORT THIS MISSION-STYLE ARMOIRE FOCAL-POINT. UNDERSCORED IN BLACK, NEW FURNISHINGS ARE CHOSEN FOR THEIR COMMON LINES, NEUTRAL COLORS, POLISH, AND WELL-MADE QUALITIES.

Although "new traditional" sounds like an oxymoron, the style is a comfortable and congruous blend of old and new, of living with timeless classics newly minted for an affordable modern life. Today you can live like the wellborn and well-bred— without the pedigree.

It's a matter of manner, an artful transition to honoring antique lines while purchasing brand-new pieces. No matter what your historic style preference, begin with a neutral, modern backdrop. Treat walls with flat paints in large, horizontal bands, choosing a paint strip that's banded in colors graduating from light to dark. Select the five lightest hues and buy a quart of each color. (Purchase paint in gallons if you're painting a large room or striping walls from room to room.) Divide the height of the wall into five sections and mark equal bands with a pencil and a carpenter's level. Fasten painter's tape above the bottom line and paint below it with the darkest color. Remove the tape and mark the next band. When the first band is dry, paint the next one; continue the process to complete the wall.

Another wall painting option: Band walls vertically with even stripes or stripes of varying widths. Expand the idea of bands to big sections of painted walls framed or interrupted by narrower bands.

Adventure onto the floor with a paintbrush, striping as shown in these open-plan rooms. Or carpet in a color that continues the bottom wall color across the floor.

NARROW, RECTANGULAR SHAPES WITH A HINT OF CURVE UNITE THIS PARK BENCH AND LANDSCAPE MIRROR. ▲

Comfortable elegance is key to new traditional dining. Choose furniture pieces that cross the boundaries between antique and modern styles.

With a neutral, modern backdrop in place, the stage is set for furniture pieces of character. The rooms in this chapter are founded on the American mission-style look that's popular in the aisles of stores that sell ready-to-assemble furniture. The first purchases placed in the shopping cart were sturdy storage pieces with "Mission" labels that established the historic style. Then came a camel-colored sofa with similar, boxy lines that looks neither Mission nor contemporary but somewhere in between.

With these beginnings in place, round out the collection with a dining set that offers sumptuous textures and curves that quietly relieve the stiff lines of the mission look and offer the open-plan space an easy elegance. A sofa table serves both sides of the room, either as a sideboard for dining or a bar for an evening in the living room. Another option: Turn a dining chair around to the sofa table for a writing desk.

With furniture and window treatments doing the transitional work of establishing a traditional style, feel free to accessorize with modern-looking fittings for tableware. Put a contemporary shine on rooms with stainless steel and sleek stemware. Bring the table down to earth with a set of stoneware dishes. Hang a mirror in a modern frame to reflect the scene.

STAYING WITHIN NEUTRAL PARAMETERS, BLACK AND WHITE TOILE SPEAKS IN A TRADITIONAL VOICE.

Dining

WIDE BANDS IN NEUTRAL COLORS SEAMLESSLY FLOW FROM WALLS TO FLOORS, ENVELOPING AN ENTIRE SPACE IN A MODERN BACKDROP. TRANSITIONAL (A BLEND OF MODERN AND TRADITIONAL) FURNISHINGS BALANCE CURVES AND STRAIGHT LINES IN A MOOD OF GENTLE FORMALITY.

169

A GRAND PLAN FOR TEXTURES TREATS THIS BEDROOM TO SMOOTHLY PAINTED STRIPES, WOOD-GRAINED STORAGE PIECES, RUSTIC WICKER, SOFT, SLUBBED LINENS, AND THE SHINE OF LIGHTWEIGHT METAL.

Sleeping

Pamper yourself with a luxury bed made with high-quality bed linens you find in the well-stocked aisles of bed and bath stores.

A MISSION-STYLE HEADBOARD AND BLANKET CHEST WRAP SOLID COMFORT AROUND A SOFTLY LAYERED BED. BLACK, THE CHOICE FOR AN ACCENT COLOR, IS DRAWN FROM THE CURTAINS AND BROUGHT INTO THE ROOM WITH TRADITIONAL BLACK LAMPSHADES ON MODERN STAINLESS-STEEL BASES.

To make a luxurious bed in new traditional style, begin by topping your mattress with a quilted pad with stretchable contour corners that keep it smooth and flat. Buy one with guaranteed stain resistance to protect your mattress. Then cover the mattress pad with a sheet (a fitted sheet stays in place better than a flat one, but a flat sheet stores more easily).

If you don't have a plush-top mattress, add a feather bed that's the same size as the current mattress top. Cover it with a protective covering or case.

Add a flat sheet. Eyptian and pima cotton are popular fabrics. For a soft, silky sheet that drapes the body, choose 100-percent-cotton sateen in 300 or higher thread count. For a crisp, cool feel, pick 100-percent-cotton percale in 180 to 250 thread counts.

The ultimate bedtime luxury —a down-filled comforter slipped inside a silken cover—is pretty enough to double as a bedcover. Check labels when purchasing the duvet. The higher the ratio of down to feathers, the more plush the comforter. (If you're allergic to feathers, choose a synthetic substitute.) Look for comforters with a 400 or more thread count to keep feathers from piercing through the shell. Compartmentalized stitching prevents feathers from shifting and eliminates the need for constant shaking to redistribute the down. Protect the comforter with a sleek, silk cover. Finish with pillows covered first in pillow protectors, then in cases to match the linens.

Details make a difference

New Torch ▲

LIGHT THE WAY WITH CUPPED SCONCES TO SIMULATE
THE MAGICAL GLOW OF OLD-FASHIONED TORCH
LIGHTS HUNG ON GRAND MANOR WALLS.

Yesterday's Time ▲

HANG A ROMAN NUMERAL CLOCK WITH WROUGHT-IRON SWIRLS TO
TAKE BACK TIME. IT FEELS GOOD TO COUNTER HIGH-TECH DIGITALS
WITH LOW-TECH ELEGANCE.

Toile Today ▲

FRAME A NEWLY PRINTED OLD-WORLD TOILE DESIGN WITH A CONTEMPORARY FRAME OR FRAME KIT. ON FABRIC YARDAGE SCREENED WITH A DISTINCTIVE OLD-WORLD SCENE, USE A STRAIGHTEDGE TO MARK THE PICTURE 3 OR 4 INCHES LARGER THAN THE FRAME'S CARDBOARD INSERT. CENTER THE SCENE ON THE INSERT AND WRAP THE EDGES AROUND TO THE BACK, FASTENING IT WITH MAILING TAPE OR DUCT TAPE. SLIDE THE INSERT INTO THE FRAME AND COMPLETE THE FRAME.

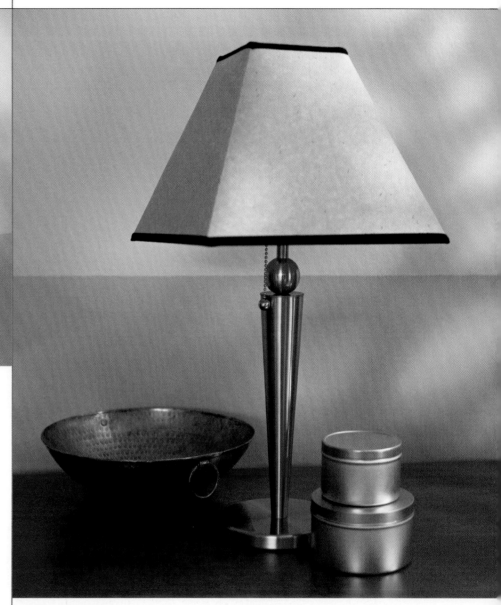

Modern Metal ▲

STEAL A LOOK. MIX ACCESSORIES OF HAND-HEWN PEWTER AND SLICK MACHINE-MADE STEEL WITH FABRIC, VELLUM, OR PARCHMENT PAPER. IT'S A SCINTILLATING BLEND OF TEXTURES.

Planning the Look

▼

COLOR Collect a feast of neutrals that speak to you in the paint stores. Note whether you prefer those with a cool blue-gray cast, those with beige-pink undertones, or those with a yellow-green vibe (khakis and green grays). The neutrals shown here tend toward the warm pink-to-yellow choices. Choose a signature (yours) accent color, such as hot pink or peach, to use judiciously.

PATTERN Collect black and tan or neutral table napkins as a start to pattern selecting. They're an inexpensive way to sample and practice transitional patterning to see how patterns look together. Another source of pattern play is to collect swatches at fabric stores that offer samples of decorator fabrics. Learn to combine geometrics and curved patterns—the neutral, black-to-cream color palette unifies a variety of patterns.

TEXTURE In a transitional scheme, it's a good idea to let a single, traditional pattern, such as toile, play a dramatic role. Textures then step into the limelight in supporting roles. Shop for surfaces to play off each other. For example, a large, traditionally shaped table lamp manufactured in streamlined stainless steel combines well with rough wicker or a dark, polished wood table. Ditto for a sleek, stainless-steel wastebasket used as a vase for hot pink peonies.

SIMPLE CURVES | GRIDDED WEAVES | WIDE STRIPES

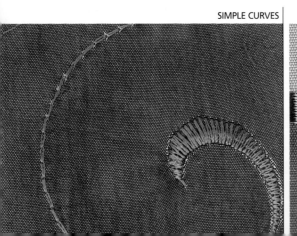
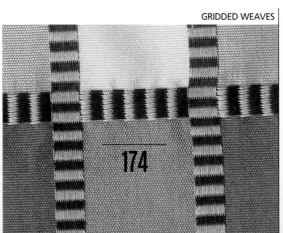
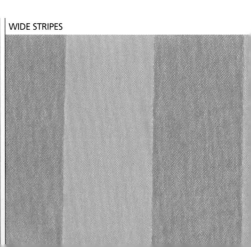

What to Shop for

FURNITURE transitional seating pieces upholstered in neutral, one-color, textured fabrics or removable slipcovers | ready-to-assemble wood armoires, chifforobes, headboards, mirrors, blanket chests, bookcases, entertainment or computer centers, and side tables | wicker, wood, wrought-iron, or steel dining chairs, bar-height stools, and armchairs | wood, wrought-iron, or glass-topped dining, side, coffee, nesting, or end tables | garden benches

WINDOW TREATMENTS pleated vellum shades | black and tan patterned side panels | standard white sheers, pleated sheers | cream or beige voile panels with beaded valances | velvet tab-top curtains | wood miniblinds

SOFT FURNISHINGS neutral silk duvet covers, sateen or charmeuse sheets and pillowcases | black and tan patterned toss pillow covers, loose upholstery cushions, tablecloths, napkins, terry cloth towels, and bath mats | one-color neutral carpeting or modular carpet tile | shag, sisal, or needlepoint rugs

TABLETOP FURNISHINGS pottery with neutral glazes | stainless-steel flatware, chargers, and barware | standard clear glasses and stemware

LIGHTING table and floor lamps with stainless-steel bases and neutral-colored shades | modern chandeliers | pendants with linen shades | pillar candles

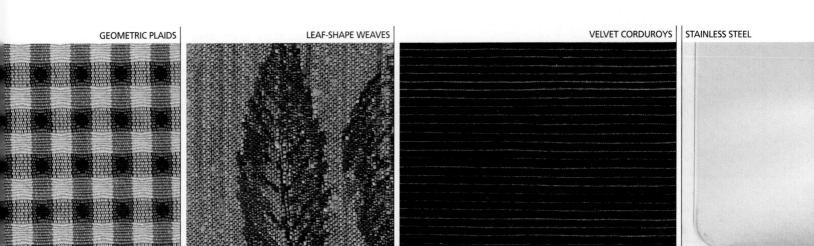

GEOMETRIC PLAIDS | LEAF-SHAPE WEAVES | VELVET CORDUROYS | STAINLESS STEEL

Bohemian

KEYS TO THE STYLE

■**RELAX, SIT BACK.** Decorating with a bohemian look is all about ignoring convention and practicing an express-yourself mode that puts a personal stamp on your rooms. If you feel the spirit, paint walls, floors, ceilings, and window frames with vivid colors or patterns. Hang flamboyant fabrics at the windows. Multiply the offbeat effect by adding big mirrors.

■**GO WITH YOUR FLOW.** This style values free expression, creativity, and furnishings that carry a sense of your personality. Never on trendspotters' lists of "what's in" or "what's out," bohemian style decorates on the cheap, taking advantage of the vast array of inexpensive mass-market buys. Unconcerned with pulling together "the right stuff," you pick and choose only the furniture pieces that get you the look you love.

■**LIBERATE FABRICS.** There are no rules. Dress up the house with tactile pieces for the sheer fun of it. Never mind what the neighbors think.

■**LESS ISN'T MORE.** Abandon the less-is-more maxim to highlight your rich flights of fancy. No scarcity of ideas resides in bohemian rooms, so trust your instincts and let your imagination fly. If collecting fascinates you and you want one-of-a-kind plates on your tables, follow the desire. If creative bargain shopping yields a bounty of nonconformist storage pieces made from baskets, boxes, and trunks, so be it. Truth be told—there's a little carefree spirit in everyone.

■**WANDER.** Markets and bazaars are the perfect place to find decorative booty: unique and colorful folk art pieces or bargains marked "as is" that you can repurpose, refinish, or repaint. Look for fake fur throws, tapestry pillows, quirky lamps, rugs, and floor screens. Collect tassels, fringes, ribbons, and passementerie trims to embellish soft furnishings. Be personal: Put photos in frames, mix hand-painted patterns, and bring the outside in with your unique choice of pots and plants.

SWIRL, STRIPE, DAMASK, SHEER, AND GEOMETRIC BARGAINS ADD UP TO EASY LIVING FOR THIS ARTIST IN RESIDENCE. DECORATING WITH FABRICS—ONE APPROACH TO CREATIVE EXPRESSION—IS SPONTANEOUS AND CAN BE CHANGED ON A WHIM. ▼

Living

Do your own thing. If slouchy slipcovers, hippie patchworks, and global imports spell living room comfort for you, go for them. Bohemian-style decorating urges vibrant lifestyles cloaked in original colorways and patterns, inexpensive furniture buys, and lots of found objects.

A likely backdrop for living bohemian style is an old house or creaky apartment with lots of quirks, aches, and pains. The advantage of these oldies-but-goodies are large spaces, antique architecture, and lots of odd nooks and crannies for storage. Besides, they're loaded with character and individuality.

These locations are often labeled "fixer-uppers"—perfect for budget-conscious free-thinkers who want to put their signatures on spaces. To do so, begin with walls and floors: Create a vibrant background for a collection of original paintings by freehanding broad painted stripes across a wall. Disguise less-than-desirable surfaces by spatter-painting across entire walls and floors, including doors and window frames. Balance walls of strong colors with more of the same, covering floors with vibrant rugs and draping windows with deep velvets and silks. Combine a series of small, mismatched rugs to cover a damaged floor. Revive high ceilings with textured wallcoverings, the kind ordinarily used on traditional wainscots. Think outside the box. Stand ordinary thinking on its ear.

AROUND-THE-WORLD IMPORTS COMPOSE A READING CORNER THAT'S DEFINED BY A DRAFT-BLOCKING SCREEN. ▲

Design dining areas for the sheer joy of combining tactile materials and serving food on a collection of objects close to your heart.

See furniture of the unfinished kind as potential for personal expression. You can turn standard ready-to-assemble pieces into original artworks with creative coverings and funky hardware. For example, a dining room sideboard of plain pine can be painted, collaged, dyed, bleached, or covered with a mosaic of broken china. Highboys, cupboards, and tables also offer generous surfaces to cover with *trompe l'oeil,* eccentric mirror and ceramic tile, or glittery gold leaf.

Cover dining tables with bargain-basement linens, layering them on for the sake of experimentation and discovering a look you love. Feast on close-out china, stoneware, or earthenware. Gather variations in colors or patterns but stick with one type of material, such as all stoneware, porcelain, metal, or glass dishes, to avoid too much disparity. Then mix in other materials when choosing flatware, glassware, and unique serving pieces.

Accent atmosphere for dining room lighting. Multiple oil lanterns, miniature electric lights, etched-glass or punched-tin candleholders, hand-painted bare bulbs, and pendant shades draped with silk scarves bring idiosyncratic points of view to your tables.

▲ A MENU OF SMOOTHIES—DAMASK, GLASS, PORCELAIN, AND METAL—BLEND WITH ROUGH CONCRETE PIECES.

FLIRTATIOUS SPIDER MUMS, PRESENTED IN RECYCLED GROCERY STORE BOTTLES, QUICKLY PROVOKE A PARTY ATMOSPHERE. GUESTS ARE SURE TO FIND MORE TOUCHABLE AND VISUAL PLEASURES IN THE COMBINATION OF SILK, VELVET, AND ORGANDY FABRICS ENHANCED BY CANDLELIGHT.

Dining

INSTINCTIVE DECORATING YIELDS SOLID DESIGN. A PREFERENCE FOR ORGANIZED PATTERNS SHOWS UP IN THIS CANOPIED ROOM. COLORS NATURALLY RELATE, TEXTURES SOOTHE, AND SIMILARLY DOTTY MOTIFS REPEAT. OLD PAPERBACKS ARE IRREVERENTLY TURNED BACKWARD ON SHELVES FOR SHOCK VALUE.

Sleeping

Bohemian-style bedrooms beg a heady blend of color and pattern, provocative textures, and out-of-the-box ideas.

TIE A RIBBON AROUND THE NECK OF AN EXOTIC FLOWER FOR A TWIST ON THE CONVENTIONAL BUD VASE.

▼ A SLEIGH DAYBED SERVES AS SOFA BY DAY AND SLEEP SPOT BY NIGHT. TO CUT AWAY THE SHORT, SLEEPING END FROM AN L-SHAPE ROOM, THEATRICAL SCRIM FABRIC IS STRUNG WALL-TO-WALL, SHOWER CURTAIN STYLE.

If you can't resist dramatic swags of fabrics in the bedroom, it's a sure sign you've been bitten by the Bohemian bug. Swept-away canopies and flowing bed curtains, curious layers of bedcoverings, and impromptu window curtains lead to improvisational sleeping lairs.

Do as you will. Although your bedroom has no practical need for a mosquito net canopy, tent a four-poster with tulle for the sheer romance of it. Filter the light atmospherically with swathes of silk and cheesecloth. Recline on a wicker chaise with loosely draped brocade coverlets and tapestry cushions. Don't stand on ceremony—flop futons on the floor to lie low when you sleep. Layer them with any number of affordable finds.

Collect gold-embroidered sari fabrics, sarongs, and Eastern bedspreads to layer on beds and wrap them with rich color and eclectic pattern. Newly made Chinese and Indian quilts are less expensive than antique or American-made quilts, so pace the aisles of import stores, bazaars, and world markets for warm bedcovers, blankets, and pillows. You'll find a wealth of irresistable batik, embroidered, tie-dyed, beaded, metallic, appliqued, and patchworked designs.

Details make a difference

Caravan Cushions ▲

SUPPORT LOOSE LIVING WITH A HIP HYBRID OF
ETHNIC DESIGN AND MODERN MANUFACTURING.
COLLECT PILLOWS AND THROWS LIKE THESE TO
SOFTEN SEATS AND WOODEN FLOORS AT SOCIAL
GATHERINGS.

Gypsy Gems ▲

BE UNCONVENTIONAL. CREATE A MAKESHIFT TABLE FROM WHAT YOU
FIND AROUND, SUCH AS THIS GRECIAN-LOOKING URN AND A GLASS
ROUND INTENDED TO TOP A PRIM DECORATOR TABLE. CONFISCATE
GLASS BEADS FROM THE GARDEN SHED TO ADD TEXTURE UNDER THE
GLASS TOP (FIRST FILL WITH STUFFING OR SAND TO SAVE ON BEAD
EXPENSES).

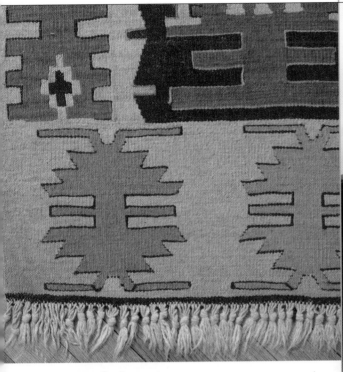

Magic Carpet ▲

DERIVE DECORATING INSPIRATION FROM
IMPORTED WOVEN RUGS. AN ESSENTIAL
COMPONENT FOR BOHEMIAN STYLE, A RUG
OFFERS COLOR SUGGESTIONS FOR OTHER
PARTS OF A ROOM, SOFTENS A FLOOR, COVERS
AN UGLY SURFACE, AND ADDS ANOTHER
LAYER OF COMFORT.

Found Object Table ▲

MAKE SOMETHING FROM ALMOST NOTHING. GIVE LEGS TO A BARGAIN-
BASEMENT BASKET WITH FOUR WOODEN FENCEPOST FINIALS FROM THE
LUMBERYARD. THE TABLE MAKES A HANDY STORAGE PLACE TOO.

Planning the **Look**

COLOR Abandon color theories and formulas for color palettes in favor of hues that feel good to you. Use your instinctive sensibilities when you step up to the paint sample rack. Once you choose an establishing hue or signature color, gather more samples, selecting a variety of colors with the same intensity, lightness, or darkness. Tip: Squint your eyes at the paint samples you choose to see if they relate closely to each other. If one jumps out, eliminate it.

PATTERN Gather wallcovering and fabric swatches to see what similarities develop (you'll have a natural tendency toward a certain type). Disparate patterns combine well if they have similar lines, colors, lightness, or darkness. In rooms filled with vibrant patterning, textures are barely noticeable.

TEXTURE If you don't want rooms dominated by effusive color and pattern, create an expressive environment by exaggerating texture. Concentrate on painting plain or spattered colors on rustic, rough-plaster walls. Mingle nappy velvets, bumpy chenilles, shiny brocades, and smooth cottons on a bed. Concoct a carpet by laying woven, shag, braided, and low-pile runners side by side. Relish a table set with a channel-stitch quilt, metallic charger plates, rustic earthenware, polished crystal, and a centerpiece of beaded fruit.

DEEP VELVET | BEADED QUILTING | VELVETY SATINS

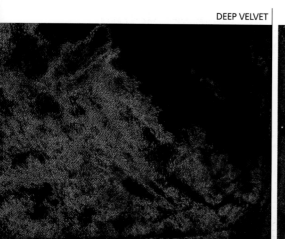

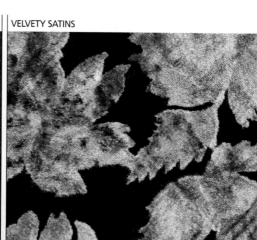

What to **Shop** for

FURNITURE bargain-basement sofas and chairs; ready-made slipcovers | unfinished and/or ready-to-assemble cabinets, bookcases, sideboards, tables, dressers, and chests | close-out sale stools, bar-height chairs, dining chairs, and floor screens | "as-is" leather armchairs, armoires, serving carts, and wicker storage trunks | improvised storage and shelving made from boxes

WINDOW TREATMENTS gold or silver lamé, ethnic printed cotton, or shimmery velveteen fabric panels hung on improvised rods | beaded drapes | scarf or bead valances | tulle, muslin, cotton, gauze, or cheesecloth sheers | Roman shades or London blinds trimmed with passementerie

SOFT FURNISHINGS faux fur and/or Mexican serape throws | theatrical bed canopies | brocade, needlepoint, patchwork, and metallic covers on pillows, beds, and floor cushions | woven rugs with indigenous patterns

TABLETOP FURNISHINGS mixed-and-matched china or stoneware in plain colors or related patterns | wood or metal trays | glasses in a multitude of colors | sari, sarong, and serape table coverings | mosaic place mats

LIGHTING beaded and fringed floor or table lamps | rope lights | flexible track lights, miniature light strings | free-form chandeliers | pendants

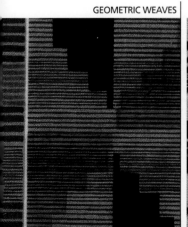

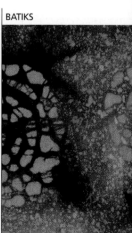

Resources

Utility Chic

PLYWOOD CHAIRS AND STOOLS, BAKER'S RACK, TV TRAY SET, UTILITY TABLES, Target Stores, 800/800-8800, www.target.com
STAINLESS-STEEL WORK TABLE, Costco, 800/774-2678, www.costco.com
GLASS TABLETOP, Pier 1 Imports, 800/245-4595, www.pier1.com
DINING CHAIRS, Crate & Barrel, 800/997-6696, www.crateandbarrel.com
WOK TOPS, EIFFEL TOWER POSTER, Cost Plus, 800/267-8666, www.costplus.com
WORK LIGHTS, BEDDING, BAR-HEIGHT CHAIRS, GALVANIZED METAL BINS, PLANT DOLLY, Ikea Home Furnishings, 800/434-4532, www.ikea.com

China Blue

PORCELAIN DISHES, DISH TOWELS, BEACH MAT, DARK WOOD TRAY, DISH DRAINER, SISAL MATS, CERAMIC TILES, Cost Plus, 800/267-8666, www.costplus.com
ARMOIRE, PAPER GLOBE LIGHTS, Pier 1 Imports, 800/245-4595, www.pier1.com
SOFA, PAPER GLOBE LIGHTS, BEDSIDE TABLE LAMP, WHITE STORAGE CHESTS, Ikea Home Furnishings, 800/434-4532, www.ikea.com
BAMBOO CHAIRS, Linens 'n Things, 800/568-8765, www.lnt.com
TIE-DYE BEDDING, Crate & Barrel, 800/997-6696, www.crateandbarrel.com
NESTING TABLES, BASKETS, FLOOR SCREEN, WHITE SHEERS, Target Stores, 800/800-8800, www.target.com

New Country

DESK, HEADBOARD, DRESSER, LINGERIE CHEST, MIRROR, Sauder Woodworking, 800/523-3987, www.sauder.com

SOFA, COFFEE TABLE, GREEN CIRCLE RUGS, RED DESK LAMP, PLANT DOLLY, SOFA CUSHION FABRICS, PENDANT LIGHTS, Ikea Home Furnishings, 800/434-4532, www.ikea.com
RAG, SHAG, AND FLOWER RUGS, COLORFUL DISHES, GREEN LINENS, BLUE QUILT, Target Stores, 800/800-8800, www.target.com
RED QUILT, SHAMS, Cost Plus, 800/267-8666, www.costplus.com

Isle Style

DIRECTORS' CHAIRS, CANE AND WICKER CHAIRS, WICKER CHEST OF DRAWERS, BASKETS, HAMMOCK, PAPER LANTERNS, COLORED GLASS VOTIVE HOLDERS, Pier 1 Imports, 800/245-4595, www.pier1.com
BAR STOOLS, LAMPSHADES, Target Stores, 800/800-8800, www.target.com
BISTRO TABLE AND CHAIRS, Ballard Designs, 800/367-2775, www.ballarddesigns.com
STRAW TOTE, TAB-TOP CURTAINS, PICNICWARE, LAMP, LINENS, Linens 'n Things, 800/568-8765, www.lnt.com
BLOCK-PRINT PILLOWS, BAMBOO BEADED CURTAIN, TOTES, LANTERNS, Cost Plus, 800/267-8666, www.costplus.com

Schoolhouse

SOFA, CHAIRS, TABLES, LAMPS, WALL-HUNG SHELVES, WALL HOOKS, BENCH, COMPUTER DESKS AND CHAIRS, WHITE ROLLING CART, Ikea Home Furnishings, 800/434-4532, wwww.ikea.com
TOWELS, PLANTERS AND LUNCH PAILS, PLYWOOD STOOLS, BEDDING, LUNCH BAGS AND BOXES, LAMINATED BOOK FILE, WASTEBASKET, Target Stores, 800/800-8800, www.target.com
RECIPE BOOK CART, GREEN BEDSIDE STORAGE, BOOK BASKETS, Pier 1 Imports, 800/245-4595, www.pier1.com

▼ **GARAGE LOCKER, METAL BINS,** Costco,
800/774-2678, www.costco.com
BLACKBOARD PAINT, Sherwin-Williams,
800/474-3794, www.sherwinwilliams.com

Greenhouse

DUVET COVER, LINENS, Bed, Bath & Beyond,
www.bedbathandbeyond.com
TUMBLED STONE TILE FLOOR, Daltile,
800/933-8453, www. daltile.com
**GARDEN BENCH CHAIRS WITH CANVAS
SEATS, TABLES, MARKET UMBRELLA, CIRCLE
PILLOWS, GREEN GLASS/BEADED CANDLE
VOTIVES,** Cost Plus, 800/267-8666,
www.costplus.com
**WICKER ARMCHAIRS, BISTRO TABLE AND
CHAIRS SET, GLASS TABLETOP,** Pier 1 Imports,
800/245-4595, www.pier1.com
**BIFOLD DOORS, PENDANT LIGHT, FENCE
SECTION FOR HEADBOARD,** Lowe's,
800/445-6937, www.lowes.com
**SISAL RUG, CHAIR THROW, TOSS RUG,
CANVAS ART, LINEN CURTAINS, LAWN CHAIR,
BAMBOO SIDE TABLE,** Ikea Home Furnishings,
800/434-4532, www.ikea.com

Soft Modern

WALL SCONCES, Lowe's, 800/445-6937,
www.lowes.com
**SOFA, CHAIRS, RUG, TABLES, STANDING
SHELF UNIT, BLUE DUVET COVER,
GROMMETED CURTAINS, CURTAIN ROD,
GLASS PLATTER,** Ikea Home Furnishings,
800/434-4532, www.ikea.com
**"SPLASH" TOWEL BAR, TEXTURED SOFA,
FLOOR AND BED CUSHIONS, SILVER PICTURE
FRAMES, WHITE PLATTER, GLASSWARE,
CERAMICS, LEATHER BOXES, FASHION
SCARVES,** T. J. Maxx, 800/283-6299
www.tjmaxx.com
**FEATHER PILLOW, SILK FRINGED PILLOW,
WHITE QUILTED BEDCOVER, SHAM, QUILTED
DUVET, POTTERY DISHES, GLASSWARE,
PITCHERS, GLASS VASES, FRUIT BOWL,** Bed

Bath & Beyond,800/462-3966,
www.bedbathandbeyond.com
NESTING TABLES, Crate & Barrel, 800/996-9960,
www.crateandbarrel.com
SPIRAL TABLE LAMP, Target stores,
800/800-8800, www.target.com
YELLOW CHAIR, Design Within Reach,
800/944-2233, www.dwr.com

Salon Style

**CAFE MARTIN LAMP, CHARMEUSE SHEETS,
STRIPED BEDSPREAD, RED RUFFLED
CUSHION, SOFA THROW,** Bed Bath & Beyond,
800/462-3966, www.bedbathandbeyond.com
LEATHER SOFA, CHAIR, Cost Plus,
800/267-8666, www.costplus.com
SECTIONAL SOFA, Design Within Reach,
800/944-2233, www.dwr.com
RED/CREAM LAYERED TABLE COVERS, KMart,
866/562-7848, www.kmart.com
BOOKCASES, Lowes, 800/445-6937,
www.lowes.com
PAISLEY RUG, CANDLES, Wal-Mart,
800/WAL-MART, www.walmart.com
FRENCH POSTERS, National Gallery of Art,
Museum Store, Washington D.C., www.nga.gov
HARLEQUIN LAMPS, ROUND DINING TABLE,
Ballard Designs, 800/367-2775,
www.ballarddesigns.com
**WICKER TABLE, END TABLES, DEMILUNE
TABLE, METAL EASEL, HANGING
CHANDELIER,** Pier 1 Imports, 800/245-4595,
www.pier1.com
**LEOPARD STOOL, WICKER/WIRE FLOOR
SCREEN, BOA-TRIMMED CANDLE LAMPS,
BEDSIDE CHEST, CLOCK, WICKER FRAME,
COAT RACK, PURSES,** Hobby Lobby,
800/323-9204, www.hobbylobby.com

Bollywood

**METAL STAR, TREE OF LIFE CANDELABRA,
GOTHIC MIRRORS, GLASS LANTERNS,
ELEPHANT TABLE, NAPKINS, PAISLEY
SARONGS, MESH LANTERN, BEEHIVE SCREEN,**

Resources

SILVER MIRROR, SILK SARONGS, Cost Plus, 800/267-8666, www.costplus.com
GOLD BLOCK-PRINTED CUSHIONS, THROWS, CANDLES, DINING CHAIRS, COFFEE TABLES, Pier 1 Imports, 800/245-4595, www.pier1.com
CUSHIONS, RUGS, BOLSTERS, FLOOR CUSHIONS, Marshalls Inc, www.marshallsonline.com

Abbey Style

BENCHES, COFFEE TABLE, WRITING DESK Cost Plus, 800/267-8666, www.costplus.com
GOTHIC MIRRORS, CROSSES, LAMPS, CANDLE STANDS, GARDEN COLUMN, BEE CATCHER, GARDEN POTTERY, "CARVED STONE" FRAGMENTS, Hobby Lobby, 800/323-9204, www.hobbylobby.com
CANDLES, CANDLE DISHES, SILVER CHARGERS, CHAMPAGNE FLUTES, LARGE MIRROR, Pier 1 Imports, 800/245-4595, www.pier1.com
WHITE FLOOR CUSHIONS, LINENS WITH CROSS EMBROIDERY, West Elm, 800/WestElm, www.westelm.com
HANGING CANDLE TRAY, Wal-Mart, 800/WAL-MART, www.walmart.com
WHITE PARSONS CHAIRS, Ballard Designs, 800/367-2775, www.ballarddesigns.com
SHEERS, WALL-HUNG SHELVES, RUG, BAMBOO TRAY, GALVANIZED BIN, Ikea Home Furnishings, 800/434-4532, www.ikea.com

Swedish Lite

STAR LIGHTS, SOFA, CHAIR, COFFEE TABLES, COLORED SHELVES, PENDANT LIGHTS, DINING TABLE, CHAIRS, BENCH, BEDDING, RUGS, DOTTED LAMPSHADE, VOTIVE CANDLEHOLDERS, Ikea Home Furnishings, 800/434-4532, www.ikea.com
BLUE BEDSIDE LAMP, CURTAINS, Wal-Mart, 800/WAL-MART, www.walmart.com
WHITE CARVED DINING ROOM SHELVES AND ALL SERVING PIECES, T. J. Maxx, 800/283-6299, www.tjmaxx.com

Loft Style

DARK WOOD MODULAR STORAGE CUBES FOR COFFEE TABLE, END TABLES, SOFA TABLE, BOOKCASE, WHITE MODULAR STORAGE CUBES FOR SOFA WRAP, COFFEE TABLE, Sauder Woodworking, 800/523-3987, www.sauder.com
DIVIDER SHELVING UNITS, FLOOR LAMP, DINING CHAIR, BREAKFAST BAR SET, SOFAS, Crate & Barrel, 800/996-9960, www.crateandbarrel.com
POSTERS, Portal Publications Ltd., www.portalpub.com, available through Cost Plus, 800/267-8666, www.costplus.com
WOOD NESTING TABLES, West Elm, 866/WestElm, www.westelm.com
LARGE DARK POTS, BASKETS, Pier 1 Imports, 800/245-4595, www.pier1.com
RUG, TABLE LAMPS, PENDANT LIGHT, BEDROOM LIGHT, PIER MIRROR, LEATHER SHAG RUG, DOWN DUVET, FRAMES, KITCHEN BOWL ART, Ikea Home Furnishings, 800/434-4532, www.ikea.com

Tuscan Sun

TERRA-COTTA/IRON PEDESTAL BOWL, BAKER'S RACK, PILLOW AND CUSHION FABRICS, FRAMES, Hobby Lobby, 800/323-9204, www.hobbylobby.com
WICKER SOFAS AND CHAIRS, WROUGHT-IRON SETTEE, BISTRO TABLE, COFFEE TABLE, LARGE URNS, DOOR MATS, CROSSBACK DINING CHAIR, Pier 1 Imports, 800/245-4595, www.pier1.com
LINEN CURTAINS, STRAW RUG, FARMHOUSE TABLE, BAMBOO BENCH, BASKETS, Ikea Home Furnishings, 800/434-4532, www.ikea.com
FARMHOUSE CHAIRS, ITALIAN PLATTERS, PLATES, BOWLS, OLIVE BOTTLES, PITCHERS, STAIR RUGS, Cost Plus, 800/267-8666, worldmarket.com
BEDSPREAD, BED AND TABLE SKIRTS, BEDDING KMart, 800/866-0086, www.kmart.com
BIFOLD DOORS, BEDSIDE LAMP, FLOOR TILES, Lowes, 800/445-6937, www.lowes.com

▼

New Traditional

ARMOIRE, LANDSCAPE MIRROR, CHIFFOROBE, HEADBOARD, BLANKET CHEST, Sauder Woodworking, 800/523-3987, www.sauder.com

NESTING TABLES, BENCH, SOFA, WICKER ARMCHAIR, WICKER DINING CHAIRS, DINING TABLE, CLOCK, PICTURE FRAMES, Pier 1 Imports, 800/245-4595, www.pier1.com

LAMPS, SHADES, SOFA TABLE, BARWARE, STOOL, Target Stores, 800/800-8800, www.target.com

RUGS, Wal-Mart, 800/WAL-MART, www.walmart.com

STEEL WASTEBASKET (VASE), POTTERY DISHES, DUVET COVER, CORDUROY PILLOW, SHEERS, CLOTH NAPKINS, Bed Bath & Beyond, 800/462-3966, www.bedbathandbeyond.com

Bohemian

PAPER GLOBE LIGHT, UPHOLSTERED ARMCHAIR, CHAIR AND BED CUSHIONS, QUILT, WOVEN RUGS, Cost Plus, 800/267-8666, www.costplus.com

LIDDED STOOLS, BEADED PENDANT LIGHTS, Target Stores, 800/800-8800, www.target.com

CARAVAN CUSHIONS, GLASS TABLETOP, GLASS BEADS, Pier 1 Imports, 800/245-4595, www.pier1.com

BEADED/PATCHWORK FABRIC, FRINGED LAMP, Hobby Lobby, 800/323-9204, www.hobbylobby.com

Credits

A SPECIAL THANKS
TO THOSE WHO PROVIDED MATERIALS, PRODUCTS, AND SERVICES

SAUDER WOODWORKING, well-known manufacturer of quality ready-to-assemble furniture, for supplying storage pieces for Loft Style, New Country, and New Traditional.

COST PLUS WORLD MARKET, for lending furniture and accessories for Greenhouse, New Country, Salon Style, Bollywood, China Blue, Abbey Style, Loft Style, Tuscan Sun, and Bohemian Style.

PIER 1 IMPORTS, for lending furniture and accessories for Salon Style, Schoolhouse, Tuscan Sun, and New Traditional.

DALTILE, A DIVISION OF AMERICAN OLEAN, for supplying the tumbled stone tile for the Greenhouse Style floor.

T.J. MAXX/MARSHALLS, for loaning pillows, rugs, storage pieces, and tableware for Swedish Lite, Soft Modern, and Bollywood.

MAGGIE ARSENAUX, for styling assistance.

SONJA CARMON, for research and styling assistance.

PEGGY JOHNSTON, for photostyling.

PHOTOGRAPHY

KING AU, pages 8-19

MARTY BALDWIN, pages 44-55

KIM CORNELISON, pages 140-151

WILLIAM HOPKINS, pages 50-51, 70, 94-95, 100-101, 108-110

SCOTT LITTLE, pages 32-43, 56-67, 80-83, 86-92, 96-99, 104-139, 152-187

WILLIAM STITES, pages 20-31, 68, 71-79, 85

Index